Feel Great

How to Manage Stress and Enjoy Life

I0210593

Jessica M Smyrl

chipmunkapublishing
the mental health publisher

Jessica M Smyrl

Published by
Chipmunkapublishing Ltd
United Kingdom

http://www.chipmunkapublishing.com

This book is dedicated to my parents who were an inspiration to me.

A big thank you to my husband Les, who has supported, encouraged and believed in me.

Jessica M Smyrl

This book is not designed to be a substitute
for professional advice. Always contact
your GP or healthcare professional
if you are concerned about your health.

Author Biography

Jessica Smyrl has had an interest in managing stress since 2006 when she studied for a Diploma in Stress Management which gave an insight into how to handle and deal with stress effectively.

She is a qualified nurse and midwife and gained a BA degree in Social Sciences and Art at the Open University. Whilst working in the NHS she studied for an MBA at Glasgow University.

She worked in the NHS and now runs health and wellbeing training and consultancy, YSM Solutions which is based in Glasgow. Her initial interest was stress within the workplace and stress in carers and this has led to the development of health and wellbeing training and consultancy company in 2009. Specialising in stress risk management, training, resilience, health coaching and wellbeing. Her current role is as a Consultant and Trainer and she is passionate about helping to reduce stress within the workplace and everyday life.

"Feel Great: How to Manage Stress and Enjoy Life" was written by Jessica as she found that many of the issues and problems which she had when working had not changed. Most of these issues are still extremely challenging for people today, so she felt that a self-help book could give some support and much needed help to all who read it.

Feel Great: How to Manage Stress and Enjoy Life

is a great resource and self-help book for anyone who is feeling under stress or is worried and anxious. There are lots of very useful tips and activities to try.

As these have helped many people, I know they work as I get feedback at training sessions, coaching sessions and during consultancy at various workplaces.

It can be read right through or picked up and used to help and support when needed. It is easy-to-use and organised in a format to help when under pressure, stress or anxious and offers information on how to reduce stress, managing your stress, immune boosters, relaxation, techniques, learn new skills, communication and organising skills.

There are useful and helpful exercises to try out, a stress diary, action plan, relaxation and more.

The shaded areas give tips and there are activities to try out.

Contents

16 Ways in Which This Book Will Help You

1. Will give you tried and tested ways to reduce and manage your pressures and stressors
2. Shows you ways to reduce worries
3. Turn criticism to your advantage
4. Be positive when challenges stretch you
5. Look and feel younger
6. Avoid feeling sorry for yourself
7. Feel and be happier with yourself
8. Embrace change and live life
9. Gives you real life experiences of how one change has empowered them
10. Give power to you
11. Feel great about yourself
12. Tells you how to relax
13. Be successful
14. How people change, and teams perform better
15. How to avoid getting emotionally upset
16. Have More Time with Good Organising Skills

Introduction

"Feel Great: How to manage stress and enjoy life" has been written to learn how you can manage your own stress at work and in everyday life. It will help with some practical information about stress, its causes, managing stress, and how to recognise signs of stress in yourself and in others. This is an updated version of Stress Management for Carers and is now perfect for all to read.

In my consultancy and training business, I meet many people from lots of different organisations, big and small. I have used my research and experience from my training and consultancy in this book from the wealth of experience I have gained over the years working as an employee and now as a trainer and consultant. It may take only one small change to make a huge difference in your life and I hope you will find it in the book.

This book will also give helpful tips and relaxation techniques and help you to learn skills and techniques to manage and reduce your stress. The book is easy to use and can be read either right through or picked up and used when there are issues which need a solution or just a quick-fix.

All the case studies are real life, but the names have been changed to protect their identity.

There are various activities throughout the book and at the back is an Action Plan to work on, as well as short and long-term goals. Aim to read through the book or pick it up when you can and then work through the activities and plans. You could start with the 'I did it' plan below.

'I did it' plan
Write down each great step you have taken whilst reading this book

No.	Great Step
1	
2	
3	
4	
5	
6	
7	
8	
9	
10	

Part One – Facts You Should Know About Stress

1

What You Should Know About Stress

Even although I had a medical background, I was not fully aware how stress could have a major impact on our bodies. Working full-time as well as caring for my mother, I found myself under stress and did not recognise my behaviour at times or did not know what to do. I starting to research the subject and found a Diploma in Stress Management course which I thought would help me and in turn help others.

At the time I was having frequent headaches and heartburn as well as a frozen shoulder which was taking a long time to improve. I did not realise that my symptoms were due to stress. It was a few years later that I realised what had caused the stress. It had been due to excessive pressure at work along with cultural and leadership issues within the organisation. This along with caring for my mother had caused my stress over a period of time. Since that time, I have made sure that I do not let stress affect me and if I do feel under stress, I now know what to do and what will help me almost instantly.

With the pace of our lives, stress is part of our everyday life and it is essential that you can recognise it in yourself and know how you can manage and cope with it effectively. Stress is affecting most of us because of the speed of life, and it is caused by too much pressure.

Stress means that we get to a certain point when we are unable to cope with pressure; this is often the case with demands at work and at home, as well as those of everyday life.

Incidents of stress are increasing, and it affects most people, with a high percentage of illnesses being attributed to stress. It can compromise the immune system, leading to more colds and infections, and over a long period of time can cause various aches and pains. These may be musculo-skeletal: painful shoulders or upper arms, sore neck, or a sore back.

There is no medical definition for stress, but this is one that clearly defines stress:

> "Stress is a threat to the quality of life and to physical and psychological well-being"
> (Tom Cox)

There is growing evidence that stress is an important factor in the development of some diseases and conditions such as high blood pressure, asthma, migraine, diabetes, insomnia, and coronary heart disease. It is important to be aware of the signs and symptoms so that you can take action before illness develops from long-term periods of stress.

A reaction to stress can be either a physical or a psychological response to a stressor, and it could be inability to sleep, anxiety, and depression. Prolonged exposure to stress is linked to anxiety and depression, as well as to physical conditions such as heart disease, back pain and headaches.

When under excessive pressure, it is important to look after yourself and in particular your emotional and physical health. A build-up of pressure can result in feeling stressed and unable to cope. There are times when you will not know what is causing the problem, but you will see as you read through this book that stress affects virtually every system in our bodies.

Work-related stress accounts for over a third of all new incidences of ill health. This can be due to many different causes which you will find later in the book.

Stress is sometimes referred to as the 'silent killer,' as it tends to be insidious to begin with and is a state of tension which is created when a person responds to the demands and pressures that come from work, family and other external sources, as well as those that are internally generated from self-imposed demands, obligations and criticism.

Stress can be cumulative and can add up over a period of time until a crisis is reached, and symptoms appear. These symptoms may manifest themselves psychologically as irritability, anxiety, impaired concentration, mental confusion, poor judgment, frustration and anger. They may appear physically as muscle tension, headaches, low back pain, insomnia and high blood pressure.

What is the Difference Between Stress and Pressure?

There is very little difference other than having adequate resources to cope with the demands placed on you. Perhaps this is why so many people talk of positive stress, when they mean positive pressure. Pressure itself is not always bad. When pressure is experienced, it can be perceived as excessive by an individual and may result in ill-health.

Working, and life in general can take their toll as they begin to feel like too much and make you feel under pressure. Excessive demands can be placed upon you, such as:

- Too much work
- Not enough time to get organised
- Targets at work
- Bills to be paid
- Appointments to keep
- Meetings
- ………………………………………..
- ………………………………………..
- ………………………………………..
- ………………………………………..

The list can go on. If you add to the above list with some of your own demands, then these demands may become excessive to the point that you feel unable to cope with the situation.

Think of a car; it can run perfectly, with the engine and everything working smoothly, but over a period of time it suffers wear and tear and its performance becomes not so good. Those who want a better performance will take it to the garage to get repaired, while others may not do anything and just leave it. If you were to continue driving, how much longer would it run for?

People are like a car in that some can perform well with some pressure, whereas others who have added pressure do not perform so well and then feel that they are becoming exhausted a lot of the time, unable to sleep or concentrate, and becoming increasingly anxious.

2
_____

How to know the Signs of Stress

What causes your stress?
Imagine building blocks and think of what could cause them to topple over. Put one on top of each other and think how many would it take before you felt under excessive pressure. These are some examples of demands or pressures on your daily life; can you add more to the examples below? If so, write them down at the next Activity and this will go towards developing your own Action Plan which you can find at Chapter 18.

Peer Pressure

Internal demands

Personality

Email, Phone

Deadlines

Activity – Causes of your Stress

```
....................................................................

....................................................................

....................................................................

....................................................................

....................................................................
```

Our personality can cause us to get more stressed and this is due to the type of personality we have. There are two types of personality: Type A and Type B.

Type A personalities can be insecure about their status and constantly trying to accomplish more and more in less and less time. They are at greater risk of developing cardiovascular disease and other stress-related conditions and can be agitated, impatient, irritable, aggressive, competitive and ambitious.

Type B personalities do not have a constant sense of urgency and have more realistic expectations. They can relax and have greater self-esteem and their expectations can surpass their own aspirations. They are patient and less competitive.

Most people exhibit characteristics of both types at different times, but they can lean towards one more than the other. For example, if you are Type A you will show some Type B characteristics, and if you are Type B you will show some Type A characteristics.

We cannot change our personality, but we can try to modify it. If you are becoming increasingly impatient and shouting, take a step back and count to ten before getting short-tempered, or leave the room for a few minutes. Go out for a walk or even go to the bathroom to calm down. Try one of the relaxing techniques at the back of the book.

The pressures of our life can be enormous, and often centre around organising your own life as well as those around you and this can mean little time for yourself. This can lead to you feeling guilty, despite the fact that you do need time for yourself.

Reduce stress by recognising the signs

There are many signs that may indicate that you or someone you know is experiencing stress. Signs of stress can be either one or a combination of physical, mental, emotional or behavioural changes.

Some of these signs may include:

Physical
- Headaches
- Unable to sleep
- Dizziness
- Blurred vision
- Aching neck, and/or shoulders
- Backache
- Chest pains
- High blood pressure

- Indigestion
- Irritable bowel
- Skin rashes
- Hair loss
- Indigestion
- Heartburn

Emotional
- Hypochondria increases
- Self-esteem falls
- Depression and helplessness
- Personality traits
- Existing personality problem increases
- Tearful

Psychological
- Anxiety
- Depression
- Concentration and attention span decreases
- Mood swings
- Motivation
- Distracted
- Lack of confidence
- Eating disorders – under or over eating
- Phobias
  - Panic
  - Addiction
  - Paranoia

Behavioural
- Critical
- Humourless
- Indecisive
- Moody
- Negative
- Aggressive
- Withdrawn

- Anger
- Fear
- Nervous ticks
- Irritable
- Clenched fists

There are many different experiences and stressors that occur in our lives which may contribute to your stress response and impact on your resilience and wellbeing. There are two types of stressors: external and internal.

External stressors or pressures can be physical conditions such as hot or cold and this could be a room that is either too hot or too cold and the impact on those around. If you work in an open plan office and one person is cold and others are hot, this can lead to problems depending on their personality which in turn can lead to stress.

Another stressor is noise which could be from a neighbour always shouting or their dog barking incessantly or loud music. Stressful psychological environments are working conditions and relationships such as bullying and intimidation.

Where there are issues at work, it is advisable to speak to a manager, HR or Occupational Health or a trade union representative. Speaking to a trusted friend or colleague can also help. When you feel that you do not wish to speak to anyone, write how you feel in a notebook or journal and as you write it down this can help to reduce the stress you feel.

Internal stressors are the way an event or experience is interpreted; an example could be that you are at home on your own and hear someone on the stairs, one of your thoughts could be that there is an intruder and the other one is that your partner has come home earlier than expected.

Another example of an internal stressor is a Type A personality and their behaviour, beliefs, attitudes and expectations, often trying to gain control within their environment can lead to frustration and anger if not achieved in the way they expect.

It is always good to be able to talk to someone you know and trust but if you don't have anyone, a support group may help. If you are not keen on either, then start a journal and write down how you feel, and by doing this, it does help to take some of the burden away.

Make notes of how you feel

3

How Stress Can Affect You

Some causes of stress are due to life events and examples are:-

Work - job insecurity / redundancy
Death of a spouse
Divorce
Marital separation
Death of a close family member
Major injury or illness
Marriage
Retirement
Moving to a New House
Financial issues

The loss of a job for some people can be the same as going through the grieving process when someone dies, and that is the loss of the life and the job you thought you would be spending most of your life working at. This can also include lifestyle such as the holidays you could have gone on and the friends that you once knew. It can take a long time to come to terms with and can lead to a lot of stress thinking that you are on your own and that no one wants to know you or even help you.

Initially, you will not feel that you want to enjoy yourself and that life is almost at a standstill and you can't see any light at the end of the tunnel. You can enjoy life again and if you manage your stress, then this will lead to a more satisfying and fulfilling lifestyle. Remember that you are important, and don't ever forget that. Relatives, friends and colleagues may help but only up to a certain point and then you need to find ways that will help you to move on and be able to enjoy life.

Our personality can cause us to become stressed as well as the way we think and perceive situations. If we have low self-esteem and lacking in self-confidence, this can be not only frustrating but cause us to be emotionally drained.

Other people can make us stressed and they fall into three different categories and you may be able to relate to them: -

1. Stress dumpers – are people who dump their stress onto others, they feel better themselves but the one they have dumped the stress onto DOES NOT.
2. Stress transmitters – are people who are stressed, and they transmit any stress they are feeling onto you and then you both are feeling uptight and stressed.
3. Stress carriers – these are people who carry their stress around with them until they eventually have a 'burnout'.

There are three stages of stress and this was identified in 1936 by Hans Selye who carried out extensive research on stress. He found that the body actually goes through three stages and these are:

1. the alarm stage
2. the resistance stage
3. the exhaustion stage

The three stages are present in any stressful activity and it is something that you need to be aware of to help to reduce its impact.

The alarm stage can be short or long and is when the stressor is appraised, and this can then lead on to the next stage. The resistance stage is when you are coping with the stressor and if this goes on for a prolonged period of time can lead to the stage when you no longer can resist, and this is what can lead to a collapse. There are very close links between psychology and physiology and this can leave you feeling exhausted physically by stress leading to psychological exhaustion. During the resistance stage, it is essential to identify the physical changes which are taking place in your body to enable action to be taken before reaching the exhaustion stage.

The next Activity will demonstrate the three phases.

Activity

Fill a glass with water and hold it in your hand with your arm outstretched as far as it can go – this is the alarm stage when you are appraising your stressor. Keep your arm in the same position without letting it come down – this is the resistance stage when you are resisting the stressor. Keep holding the glass at arm's length and eventually, you will not be able to hold it any longer and this demonstrates the exhaustion stage.

In the 1960s, two American psychologists, Thomas Holmes and Richard Rahe, developed a scale of 43 life events considered to be stressful, and it was called The Holmes-Rahe Social Adjustment Scale. They were then ranked in order of the amount of stress associated with each event as follows:-

Death of a spouse/partner		100
Divorce		73
Marital separation		65
Marriage		50
Retirement		45
Pregnancy		40
Moving house	20	
Holiday		13
Christmas		12

Are there any surprises in the above list? Times have not changed much as far as the above list is concerned as these will possibly be the same or very similar today. One big change is the volume of cars on the road and this can lead to problems such as road rage. Trolley rage occurs in the supermarket and queue jumping can cause big problems for anyone in a hurry.

How Stress Hormones Affect You

There are three main stress hormones: noradrenalin, or the fight mode, adrenaline, the flight mode, and cortisol, which work with noradrenalin and adrenalin. The 'fight or flight' or stress response is a reflex reaction to a perceived danger or threat and this can be psychological or physical.

When under stress, adrenaline is present in the blood and causes blood pressure to rise and additional fuel (glycogen or sugar) and oxygen required by the bloodstream, plus an increased blood supply going to the muscles and the heart. The body is therefore able to respond to stress by flight or by fight. The adrenals are sometimes referred to as the 'glands of flight and fight' or the emergency glands. Noradrenaline affects the circulation mainly by contracting the blood vessels and raising blood pressure.

Adrenaline and Noradrenaline play different roles in preparing the body for action. Some of the changes are that the digestive system slows down considerably; there is improved visual perception, increased muscle tension and blood pressure, blood sugar and cholesterol are higher with an increase in respiratory and heart rates.

Adrenaline

Most people have heard of adrenaline. It helps the body prepare to get away from danger or the 'flight' mode. The heart rate increases, and the heart can be felt beating fast and it can become erratic and sometimes described as palpitations. The blood supply to all vital organs and muscles increases which in turn causes a reduction in the blood supply to the digestive system and this can make the stomach feel as if it is churning or like butterflies. Sweat can then appear on the skin with a feeling like a 'cold sweat' going over you. Adrenaline can make us forget things; reduce our concentration which results in difficulty making decisions.

Noradrenaline

Noradrenaline is not so commonly known with the response being opposite to Adrenaline. Noradrenaline is thought to be the precursor of adrenaline, but it is not present in such large amounts as adrenaline.

Noradrenaline is the 'fight' response and can become more aggressive with tension in the face, muscles become tense and this causes contraction of the blood vessels and blood pressure being raised. The pupils of the eyes dilate, and it helps you to be more alert mentally resulting in quick decision making and can even leave you with a feel-good feeling. There is more detail of what happens to our bodies in Chapter 6.

Nowadays, there are very few occasions when we have a physical response to get out of danger and an example of this could be hitting a door or a post when we don't see it or are not looking. We 'get a big fright' and quickly move out of the way, our heart starts racing with the surprise, breathing increases and our muscles are tense. How often does this happen to us? We do not have many, if any, physical stressors. However, our body does not know the difference between a physical and a psychological stressor, so the response is the exact same. If this happens over and over in one day due to a psychological stressor, think about the wear and tear on your heart, lungs and other organs. Over a period of time, it will have an impact on your body and on your health.

Some of the signs of the *Fight or Flight* response are:-

- Increased heart rate
- Increased breathing
- Muscles tense
- Pupils dilate
- More sweat
- Mouth goes dry
- Digestion slows

When under stress, this response can occur several times a day, and if that is the case, effective action requires to be taken. It can be insidious, so it is important that you are aware of what is happening to your body under certain circumstances. This will give you an indication of how often it is occurring, and that you do need to act to prevent or avoid it.

Rest and relax. It is always good to have some specific time so that you can rest your body after a long and exhausting day both mentally and physically. You are often more tired than you realise, so sit on a comfy chair and put your feet up on a stool and maybe listen to some soothing music or read a book.

Next time you think you are showing signs of the stress response or feeling very tense, take a note of it in the

Stress Diary in Chapter 16. This will identify if there is a pattern by dates, times and your reactions, such as being unable to speak as your mouth is so dry.

Sleep Deprivation and Stress Symptoms

Interestingly, the Symptoms of Sleep Deprivation are also the Symptoms of Stress which you can see at Fig. 1.

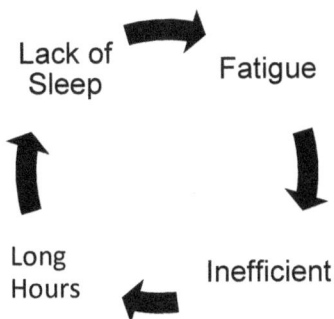

Lack of Sleep → Fatigue → Inefficient → Long Hours → (back to Lack of Sleep)

Inefficiency Circle Fig 1

Fig 1 demonstrates that sleep deprivation is also symptoms of stress

Acknowledge any signs from your body and 'listen to your body'. For example, if you have a headache, is it due to not taking enough fluids or are you suffering from a migraine which could be due to a build-up of tension?

You accept that you are feeling under pressure or stressed. If you accept it, then you can take positive action to deal with the stress.

Notes about how you feel just now

4
_____

How Stress Can Affect You at Work

If you are working full or part-time, and feeling under stress, then make sure your manager has completed a Stress Risk Assessment. Every organisation and all their managers' have a 'duty of care' to their employees. Below are some statistics relating to Stress at Work: -

- Work-related stress accounts for over a third of all new incidences of ill health.
- Each case of work-related stress, depression or anxiety related ill health leads to an average of 30.2 working days lost.
- A total of stress, anxiety and depression resulted in 11.7 million working days lost at an estimated social and economic cost of £5.2 billion

The Health and Safety Executive Management Standards can be found on their website and are guidance. However, employers already have duties under the following:-

- Management of Health and Safety at Work Regulations 1999: To assess the risk of stress-related ill health arising from work activities.
- Health and Safety at Work etc Act 1974: To take measures to control that risk.

So often it is found that the legal aspects do not appear to have any impact on some organisations! However, there is the potential of enforcement action which could be taken by the Health and Safety Executive (in the UK) on work-related stress in some circumstances.

Research has shown work-related stress to have adverse effects for organisations in terms of: -

- Employee commitment to work
- Staff performance and productivity
- Attendance levels
- Staff recruitment and retention.

Set personal goals to manage pressure and increase your performance

If you can set goals it helps to prioritise what is important for you to achieve something in your life.

Identify time for you. It can help to motivate you plus building your self-confidence.

If you don't already set personal goals, start now so that when you achieve a goal, you can give yourself a pat on the back or reward yourself and it gives you a motivational boost.

All employees should have an awareness of the factors that cause stress and take on board suggestions which will help them. Managers can do a great deal especially by giving support and guidance as well as, if appropriate, being referred to a Stress Management Practitioner (an option to counselling) or in some instances to a Counsellor.

When there are any issues, it is best to approach a Manager so that the issue is resolved by dealing with it quickly and proactively. By tackling stress early, there is much less chance of employees taking time off sick which costs the company both in lost productivity and impacts on profits.

If you are a manager, it is advisable managers are trained by stress management specialist trainers, to enable them to identify symptoms and be able to manage stress within the workplace. They could indicate that there is cause for concern in individuals and this will help any organisation proactively combat stress. In extreme cases if an individual claims work-related stress has caused them to be off on long-term sick, an organisation can feel severely disadvantaged if the individual brings a case against them and wins.

Nowadays, pay outs for stress-related illness can be considerable and many ends up as out of court settlements, and this is a way whereby the organisation will not be in the press which could be extremely detrimental to them.

It is vital that managers can identify and be able to recognise stress, resulting in helping and supporting employees to deal with it effectively and proactively which ensures that they help to protect their organisation from potential claims. This will result in a healthier and happier workforce.

Tackling stress does bring business benefits. There are many benefits when stress is managed effectively and here are some benefits: -

- ✓ Reduce accidents
- ✓ Reduce sickness
- ✓ Improved financial performance
- ✓ Improved customer satisfaction
- ✓ Improved employee satisfaction
- ✓ Improved performance and quality
- ✓ Increased productivity
- ✓ Improved work / life balance

Case Study

I was approached by a company to carry out a full Stress Risk Assessment due to high levels of sickness absence due to stress and stress-related conditions.

After a meeting with members of the Board, the agreed approach was to deliver Stress Awareness and Wellbeing training sessions for all employees rather than a survey. This was because there were not sufficient staff to ensure that it was anonymised – most staff could be identified due to where they worked. Valuable feedback was gained from the sessions and I had agreement from the employees and management to enable me to provide feedback to the senior management team which was all anonymised.

Good management and good work within an organisation are the best ways of stress prevention. It is important for organisations to identify and deal with any stress problems and continuously monitor for stress issues as well as promoting a healthy workplace which can help to reduce and prevent stress.

Following the training sessions, I provided a report to the Board and gave recommendations which included in-depth training for all managers on how to manage and reduce stress in the workplace, carry out individual stress risk assessments, improve communications, identify a Health and Wellbeing Champion. These were some of the recommendations and a few months later, the Company agreed to carry out the sessions for all managers to attend.

This did help the managers to identify stress early and in turn reduced sickness absence levels, improved productivity and performance.

So often I hear that people are not getting the support they need, and you do need support from the team you work in as well as your manager. This could be working more flexibly even for a short time until you feel under less stress. You may have access to counselling through your employer if this would help you. Otherwise, have a look at some of the tips in the book.

Always seek medical advice when stress is prolonged, or you are feeling unwell due to stress.

3 Quick Tips to Reduce Stress

1. Alter the situation

2. Avoid the situation

3. Accept the situation

What 3 quick steps could you take? It is amazing when you can take a step back from your situation as if you were looking through a camera lens at yourself. You will see things in a different light and make the list and act on it.

Openness of how you feel. *Tell yourself and those around you that you are feeling stressed. Possibly everyone around you knew before you did!*

5
_____

Bullying Can Be Happening to You and You Don't Even Realise

One of the most common types of bullying is peer to peer bullying or horizontal bullying and this is when one colleague bullies another colleague and upwards bullying is when a manager is bullied by a member of their team.

I carry out training for the Royal College of Nursing (RCN) members as I am an RCN Associate Consultant and Trainer. The training has taken me all over Scotland and there continues to be a growing problem of bullying within the workplace. This is in all sectors and not just the public sector. I also provide bullying training onsite and as open courses as it is a growing problem and many people do not know what to do or where to go for help.

Downward bullying

This is when, for example, a manager bullies a subordinate. This can be giving them work that they do not have the skills to carry out or giving them so much work that they are unable to complete any within the timescale asked for. In other words, 'setting them up to fail'.

An incident happened within the NHS when a manager was giving one of her team (Amy – not her real name) work that she had no skills to carry out. Amy could not say she was unable to do the work and this set her up to fail with devastating impact on Amy. One day she left work in tears and the next day the manager started shouting at her as she said that she had done something wrong even although Amy tried to explain that it was a genuine error and was not obvious at the time. The manager had shouted at Amy when no one else was in the department.

Amy did nothing about this manager but decided to leave the organisation as she did not feel anyone would listen to her. In time, her health improved, and she was successful in another area of the private sector.

Upward Bullying

This is when a team member bullies a manager, and this is often that they resent being told what to do and make life extremely difficult for the manager.

I have found this form of bullying to be more common than I realised, and this is from my research to carry out training and consultancy.

Case Study

A care home manager was recently telling me after a training session that she was being bullied by a clinical support worker and the impact it was having on her daily life was unbelievable. The manager was tearful and had not discussed it with her partner at home, although difficult for the partner not to notice that something was not right.

The support worker was aggressive and constantly rude to the manager who was at the stage she was unable to deal with the situation as it had affected her psychological health to such an extent that it had caused her to lose her self-confidence and self-esteem.

I suggested that she contact her free counselling service which was available for her to access. She did not realise that she could access the service and was going to that evening.

The manager did say to me that HR were currently supporting her, but it was taking a considerable amount of time. She was delighted to report the following week that the clinical support worker was leaving, and the future appeared to be getting much brighter for her.

This one change was going to make a big difference to the manager's day to day life, but I did say that it would take time and counselling to get her back to her more confident self. By helping herself with new skills and training herself to be positive would help her over time.

Overt Bullying

Bullying can be overt, and some examples are shouting or swearing at staff or colleagues either in public or private. Some other examples can be 'speaking down' to a colleague in front of others, being critical and sarcastic on a regular basis.

Covert Bullying

Another form of bullying is covert, and this can be taking the credit for someone else's work, spreading malicious rumours, ignoring, interrupting every time you make a comment especially at meetings, not giving someone enough work to do and giving impossible targets and timescales.

If It Is Happening to You

It is best to speak to the bully but only if you feel confident to do so. Why should you let this individual shout at you? 'No way' you say.

I would suggest that you say to the bully 'please do not shout at me again' and they may be taken aback as they didn't realise this. If on the other hand, they continue then it is a case to repeat the sentence a few times until they get the message. They may not get the message and it is best to take it further.

It is very useful to keep a diary of date, time, what was said to you and how it was said or what actions, how did it affect you, what were your actions and was there anyone else present as a witness. Keep this diary and if you are in a trade union or professional body such as RCN, then speak to a representative.

You may also talk to a manager or HR and if it is your manager bullying you, then speak to their manager.

As bullying is very stressful, it can be useful to attend counselling which is available for members of professional bodies and trade unions as well as some workplaces offering it. Counselling is entirely confidential, and no one will know that you have contacted the service unless you tell them yourself.

The saddest story I heard was when I was carrying out Bullying Training for Nurses and at the end of the session a nurse came up to speak to me. She told me that she was from Rwanda and was being bullied by her peers at work. She loved her job nursing and was finding it intolerable. She had seen her family brutally killed in the 1994 Rwandan genocide and she had survived that only to come to the UK to be bullied.

I was almost in tears when she was speaking to me as I couldn't believe how cruel people can be especially nurses who are in a caring profession. I listened and advised her to speak to the RCN or trade union and gave contact details and was able to point her in the direction of local representatives.

> *"Do not judge me by my success, judge me by how many times I fell down and got back up again."*
> *~ Nelson Mandella*

Part Two – How Stress Can Impact on You

6
_____

How You Will Know What is Happening to Your Body When Stressed

When I was studying for my Diploma in Stress Management I went back to read some of my anatomy and physiology student nursing books.

Our bodies are fantastic, and I always say at my training sessions to be aware of our bodies and to 'listen to your body'. When we have a headache or stomach pains on a regular basis, think why is this happening and is there a reason. What is the trigger? Even take a note of what is happening such as date, time, symptoms, who you were speaking to or at a meeting for example and see if there is a pattern and it may surprise you. This has worked many times and I have had good feedback.

When there is any psychological or physical challenge; major or minor, a part of our brain causes the release of adrenaline, which is one of the stress hormones, into the blood. If it is a physical response, such as if we are not looking where we are going and bump into a lamppost, we very quickly can get out of danger and then everything slows down and gets back to normal.

A psychological response due to bullying behaviour, for example, will have the same reaction as physical and this can be occurring several times in a day. At this point, some of our organs in our body are put on full alert. Adrenaline provides our bodies with the strength, energy and clear thinking necessary to meet whatever the challenge is. Our body's reaction is the same if it is physical or psychological, this would mean our heart rate increases, blood pressure increases, breathing rate increases, sweating more, your mouth going dry and pupils dilate.

Adrenaline causes raised blood pressure with an extra supply of glucose or sugar and oxygen into the blood stream, also an increased blood supply to the muscles and heart. This enables the body to respond to stress by the 'fight or flight' mode. Noradrenaline affects the circulation, contracting the blood vessels and raising the blood pressure. More details around the hormones are in Chapter 3.

The effects of stress can affect many parts of the body and stress will inhibit gastric secretions, and indigestion can occur from rushing meals and not taking time to eat a meal properly. Gastric and duodenal ulcers can be exacerbated by lifestyle. Stress inhibits the secretions of mucous which would normally protect the stomach or duodenal wall from acid. This can result in the acid burning a hole in the wall and can lead to an ulcer. Similarly, stress can either inhibit acid production or stimulate it. In the latter case, this excess acid can burn holes in the stomach lining, resulting in an ulcer. A reduction in secretion, of the protecting mucous will also cause stomach acid to burn the wall of the stomach and may result in an ulcer. Research used to show that stress was always implicated in gastric ulcers but is more often linked to Helicobacter pylori bacteria.

The stomach is where we digest our food and where we get our sustenance. Do you think the statement "you are what you eat" is an accurate one for you? We need to make sure that all food we eat is well cooked and it is not past its sell by date. We all have a different level of sensitivity to different foods and this can be the case for very spicy foods as they can create a high level of acidity in the blood. Other foods that cause a high level of acidity in the blood is hard cheeses, red meats and coffee.

There are times when we feel that we are lacking in energy or feeling tense when under pressure or stress that we tend to want to eat these types of foods. At this time, our digestive system is not working as efficiently, and this can lead to problems digesting them well. As a result, there can be an increase in acidity in the blood, and this can cause blood pressure to be raised. When you are under stress, it is advisable to eat foods which can be easily digested so try and avoid rich and spicy foods.

It is important to take time to eat your food and if you eat too quickly and don't take time even to taste it; this can lead to indigestion and weight gain. Try not to eat food too quickly as this means that you don't enjoy the food when you eat quickly and will lead to getting hungry quicker. By eating slowly, this allows you to chew food slowly and be able to taste the different flavours, improve digestion and also feeling more relaxed. Eating at a table is essential for a relaxed meal and enjoying company helps to relax and it will improve your immune system also which is vital when under stress.

Aim to eat five fruit and vegetables each day. These should include, citrus fruits, green vegetables and of course potatoes. Vitamins are essential to take when under stress especially Vitamin C and Vitamin B complex.

A key to fighting stress is one small change and this can be done by creating a list of small changes or just one change that you would like to see make a big difference in your working or home life.

An example could be that you are going to walk to get the newspaper in the morning rather than taking the car or walk to post a letter. This will leave you feeling better as you have had some exercise and got some fresh air into your lungs. When you return home, you will feel more invigorated and ready for the day ahead. Change your daily commute, take a different route to your usual one, or go and visit a place you have never been before. Think about some changes you would like to make TODAY and jot them down.

I would like to change...and

....

and ....

....

....

How Stress affects the Immune System

A healthy immune system is essential to good health, emotionally, physically and psychologically. When you are busy with little or no time for yourself, the immune system can become weakened because of stress and fatigue and lack of sleep.

The immune system is the body's natural defence against disease and it is like an invisible army or a barrier defending the body from infections and bacteria all the time to keep you fit and healthy. It consists of a complex network of specialised cells which help to defend the body against bacteria and viruses, and it can also fight cancers. An immune system is essential so that you do not succumb to disease.

The effect of prolonged stress is suppression of the immune system by cortisol, which is one of the stress hormones, and it is produced by the adrenal glands, which can lead to a weakened immune system. The

Adrenal glands are two small triangular glands which lie over each kidney. When there is an excess of cortisol, it can decrease the number of circulating lymphocytes and eosinophils (these are the blood cells which help to fight infection) and this can then lead to a reduction in the production of antibodies which help to fight infection.

When the immune system is weakened, this can result in more infections and you can end up having more colds and flu. The body can also become more susceptible to immune system related diseases such as asthma, rheumatoid arthritis, cancers and allergies.

I was speaking to managers in a local company who had a fairly high level of sickness due to stress. I did say to them that the amount of people off with other conditions could also be stress-related as not everyone wishes to say that they are off with stress.

An example could be musculo-skeletal conditions which can be due to a huge amount of tension in the body and the person is not able to relax. Other examples can be raised blood pressure but there could be other reasons for this. However, it did give them some food for thought and it is useful to check to see what people are off with over a period of time to see if there might be a connection.

I went to Spanish classes last year and it did completely focus the mind on learning the language and looking forward to the next class and getting the homework done! It is a good way to meet other people as well as having the confidence to speak a different language.

Try something new.

Something you could think of doing is to go for long walks or even joining a walking group. You could start a new hobby, and this is also a way to meet new people, examples could be painting, cookery, yoga or learn a language.

Write down your thoughts.

7

Reduce your Worries and be More in Control

How you can worry about small things?

We all worry about different things. Some people say they are born worriers. Whereas others worry about what they said to someone or what they are going to do next. So often we can worry about what is outwith our control. With 50,000 to 70,000 thoughts per day, you can use up a lot of energy, so it is better to use it efficiently than inefficiently.

You may worry about your health or how to cope with various situations; major upset or change in circumstances, moving to a new area or a new job or losing your job.

With worry comes fear and often it is fear of the unexpected. Sometimes worry about your job whether there will be changes, and then you could lose your job. This is out of your control so what I say at training sessions is to make two lists – one of what you can control and one that you cannot control. The list of what you cannot control, leave and focus on what you can control.

I ran a training session for a global company who were making some of their employees redundant. One of the attendees asked me how she could take control and I said to look at change as a challenge and an opportunity to do something new or maybe completely different such as learning new skills, developing current skills, look at transferrable skills, a completely different career, or starting up your own business. The main thing I always say is to focus on what you can control and once you realise there is nothing you can do over what is out of your control, then do not to use your energy over this, it can make you more worried or concerned and it is best to put your focus on what you can control.

When I was at a networking event, I was speaking to a woman who had worked in a local council as an accountant. She had been made redundant and got divorced around the same time. It had been a very stressful time for her, but she decided to train to be a sports therapist and said that she had not looked back since. She was very positive and happier about the future and was now looking for a new house.

Have a think about 3 activities that will move your actions, thoughts and energy from what you cannot control to what you can control. Take note of how you feel and how your attitude has changed, and your energy level has increased.

1.

2.

3.

*"I never worry about action, but
only about inaction."*

– Winston Churchill

From the bible, Jesus said "Take therefore no thought for the morrow: for the morrow shall take thought for the things of itself".

Willis H Carrier who invented modern air-conditioning had a formula as described by Dale Carnegie. This is something that would be useful to try out when you are worrying. It did work for him and he became very successful.

- *Step one*: Ask: What is the worst that can possibly happen?

- *Step two*: Prepare to accept it mentally.

- *Step three*: Then calmly proceed to improve on the worst.

Carrier had said

"I was stunned by my failure. It was almost as if someone struck me a blow on the head. My stomach, my insides began to twist and turn. For a while I was so worried I couldn't sleep.

Finally, common sense reminded me that worry wasn't getting me anywhere; so I figured out a way to handle my problem without worrying. It worked superbly. I have been using this same anti-worry technique for more than thirty years".

Step 1. Analyse the situation fearlessly and honestly. Figure out what's the worst that could possibly happen as a result of the failure or situation.

"No one was going to jail me or shoot me. That was certain. True, there was also a chance that I would lose my position; and there was also a chance that my employers would have to remove the machinery and lose the twenty thousand *dollars* we had invest".

Step II. After figuring out the worst that could possibly happen, accept it if necessary.

"I said to myself: This failure will be a blow to my record, and it might possibly mean the loss of my job; but if it does, I can always get another position. Conditions could be much worse; and as far as my employers are concerned – well, they realize that we are experimenting with a new method of cleaning gas, and if this experience costs them twenty thousand dollars, they can stand it. They can charge it up to research, for it is an experiment".

Step III. From that time on, devote your time and energy to improving upon the worst which you have to accept mentally.

"I probably would never have been able to do this if I had kept on worrying, because one of the worst features about worrying is that it destroys your ability to concentrate".

If you have a current situation you are worrying about, try the formula and see how you get on.

When you are worried, you may be unable to sleep. What I find does work is to go to bed at the same time each night and get up at the same time each morning, regardless how you feel, and this can help to get into a pattern resulting in better sleep. It helps to persevere for about two weeks.

Case study

Several years ago, I was carrying out training sessions for carers and they were over half days. I was running a Stress Management for Carers locally which were very popular, and Anne (not her real name) was one of those who attended both sessions. She looked after her husband who had been an academic and was now bedridden.

Anne was exhausted and looked tired, her hair was limp, and her overall demeanour was not good.

I had been talking about all the causes of stress and how it can impact on our physical and psychological wellbeing.

The next time I saw her about two weeks later, I hardly recognised her, and I had to say that she looked well. She replied that she did not feel worried about all the ailments she had as she knew that it was now stress-related.

Anne's hair looked shiny and a different style and she looked as if the weight of the world had been taken from her shoulders. She did accept that she still had to care for her husband, but she had to be fit and well, so essential not to be worrying so much and to take care of herself.

This had made Anne look a lot younger and feel happier in herself. The fact that she was no longer worrying about her health and her current situation. She took on board what she could change and embraced it. What she could not change, she had to accept and look at ways to improve her own lifestyle.

Think about your situation and write down how you could make even one small change which would make a huge difference to you.

8

Getting to Know Yourself

Any success in dealing with life stress must begin with self-knowledge and there are some things you can't change such as your current job or a situation. In time you can change it possibly. Self-knowledge brings awareness that you can alter your perceptions, lifestyle, behaviour or your situation to cope more effectively with stress.

> *"If you ask what is the single most important key to longevity, I would have to say it is avoiding worry, stress and tension. And if you didn't ask me, I'd still have to say it."*
> *– George F. Burns*

Activity

Monitor what is causing stress and note how you feel at that time and the level of stress. When you are monitoring stress levels, this can help you to become more objective of monitoring your progress and give yourself a treat for the improvement.

Tip: there is a Stress Diary at the back of this book.

Some Methods to Avoid!

Some of the methods which you may have tried to manage stress have long-term side effects which can end up leaving you with worse side-effects than the original problem. These methods will deal with the symptom short-term but will not solve the problem. However, some people do feel that this is the best course of action for them and if this is what you are thinking about, have a word with your GP.

When stressed, smoking can increase and with the pressure of your current role can lead to drinking a lot more alcohol than usual due to possibly not sleeping and feeling listless and tired. Other self-administered drugs can be caffeine, solvents and illegal drugs. More problems, of course, can occur when used on a regular and excessive level.

Overeating or under eating can be problematic, as physical signs of stress can lead to obesity or eating disorders such as anorexia nervosa or bulimia.

OCD – Obsessive Compulsive Behaviour can become exacerbated by stress especially if there are problems at work, for example, such as always checking to see if a door is locked or looking at your watch every minute or more often.

Becoming angry or aggressive with those around you or your loved ones doesn't help you or those about you and this can lead to more stress and problems.

> *Try some alternative methods today! It is easier than you think, and you will feel so much better in yourself.*

Jessica M Smyrl

You should have identified what your stressors are, and if not, have a think about what is causing you to become stressed. Think about your current role and what is causing you to get stressed over the past week. Make a quick list or just think of one factor at a time.

To help to manage your stress, some factors can be changed by changing the environment by adding, removing or re-organising it and this could be getting some help or support to allow you to go out to meet friends, to go for a walk or to go shopping. Changing your behaviour can improve relationships with others and this can help by improving communication skills. You may decide that instead of working full-time, that part-time would be a better option all round. If you do not work, it could be taking time out for yourself.

When you are busy juggling everyday life, it is important to be able to set priorities by planning your time effectively and using time in a more positive and effective way. You can do this by marking in your diary or a calendar that on a certain day of the week you are going to go out for a long walk, to meet friends or go for a meal. It is up to you to make sure that you put something down each week and when you see it written down, you then begin to look forward to it and this can give you a more positive approach to life. Try it and see how you get on.

Use stickers with positive thoughts and put in a prominent place such as a mirror, drawer or car. Put a few words or a word such as "I am great", "be positive", "I can do it" on a sticker and the more often you see the words, the more you believe it and you then feel a lot better with the situation.

There are many times when we do not feel like being positive, but the more you see it and try it the more real it becomes.

There is no fun in being negative all the time, it doesn't help you so be positive and take action now.

Finding out about yourself

Effective stress management means finding your own optimum stress level, the point of balance at which the body and mind function best. This varies with each person and the task.

I always aim to have a lunch break away from my computer or if I am training, ensure that it is put into the programme. Aim to take a break whether you are working or not and make sure that you are not having a break or lunch sitting at a computer.

It is good to get some fresh air and exercise. If you stay at the computer all the time, how productive are you? It is amazing the difference that getting up and walking maybe round the block or to the shops can make you feel.

I frequently hear 'I am far too busy to take a break' and I have deadlines to meet. If this is you, then do a different task for a short time as you are using a different part of your brain. Then return to the original task which may have helped you to think clearer.

Case study

Recently, I was speaking to Rebecca who had started having severe headaches to the extent that it was becoming migraines and she could not work. She had been working 12-hour days which may be okay for a short time, but it was going to have an impact on her overall health in time. She wasn't taking lunch or tea breaks.

I suggested that she look at when she started work and when she finished and to make sure that she worked her contracted hours, had a tea break and was away from her desk for lunch. I asked her to keep a migraine diary as well as her start and finish times.

I reviewed her in two months' time and she was able to report that she had not had any more severe headaches or migraines and felt a lot better in herself with more energy and she felt happier as well she said. This was having an impact on her work and her home life.

Rebecca did realise that she had to take care of herself or the next time it could be a lot worse. She also had to be firm with herself to keep to her working hours. She did admit as a senior manager she had a lot of pressures and she had discussed this with her manager who was supportive to her and was taking some of her workload away from her which had helped in her recovery.

Do you like exercising or would you prefer another option?

Maybe not but it is good to have an exercise programme that you can stick to. If a strict regime is what you are thinking about, such as going to the gym and pounding on the treadmill, plus weights and other activities, then give it a try. However, there is another option if you feel that the gym would be a short burst and then it cannot be sustained.

The secret here is to make sure it is something that you can sustain, and you are happy and willing to do. When you go to the supermarket, park the car at the farthest away corner and this gives you some exercise walking to and from the supermarket. It can be difficult when you are working or a busy lifestyle to get time to go to the shops, but this will help with shopping and make you feel a bit better about yourself. You also won't forget where you parked your car as it will possibly be one of a few cars as this is what I do as I need to practice what I teach! Even when you are sitting, you could try some exercises such as getting a stress ball in your hand and squeezing it. This helps your wrist and hand be more flexible and can lower the risk of injury.

Walking around the house and walking up and down stairs can help or go into the garden and do some gardening or walk around the garden. Not only are you getting some exercise, but you are getting fresh air. Any form of exercise is good for us as endorphins are released into the body leaving you with a feel-good feeling.

Getting to know yourself and your personality is something that you need to seriously have a think about. Have you decided if you are more a Type A or a

Type B personality? You cannot change your personality, but you can try and modify it. Have you thought of steps you can take to modify it yet? If not, have a think and if you cannot think of anything, write down how you are feeling in your Stress Diary section, and this could give you an indication where you need to take some positive action.

To make sure you have success in dealing with stress in your life, it is best to start with self-knowledge. There are some things you can't change, e.g. current role but self-knowledge brings awareness that you can alter your perceptions, lifestyle, behaviour or your situation to cope more effectively with stress. You can do this yourself, but you could get support from a Stress Management Coach or Practitioner who would work with you and develop a Stress Management programme over a six-week period tailored to meet the specific needs of the individual.

Balance is the key, and balance means that we create an improved lifestyle.

Activity
What is the difference between good methods for handling stress and bad methods for handling stress?

Make a list of methods you can think of and decide which side you are on now, and then add them up.

Good	Bad

Feel Good Notes ☺

9

How to Improve Your Wellbeing

Recognise and know how you react when you are under stress and take a note of changes in your behaviour such as getting angry and impatient with those you work with or those you love. It is important to have a strong network of friends or a good support group to be able to talk and to relate to others in a similar situation to your own.

Stressed? Then lose it – Take action NOW!

Remember stressed in reverse is desserts and, like a dessert, a little is okay, but a lot is NOT.

Thinking positive thoughts is also important. See Chapter 15.

Watch your diet – aim for well-balanced

It is essential to have a well-balanced diet including fruit and vegetables and make sure that you have a good meal at least once a day.

Take time to eat and enjoy your food by using your senses, so look at the different colours, smell the aromas and appreciate what you are going to eat. Take each mouthful slowly, chewing over in your mouth and this allows for more saliva which will help with the digestive processes.

When you are under stress, there are some vitamins and minerals that are reduced, and this is due to suppression of the immune system by the stress hormone cortisol, so it is important to ensure you take adequate vitamins such as Vitamin B Complex (these can be bought in tablet form but check with your GP first). The minerals which are reduced when you are under stress are zinc which is required for healing tissue, and iron which is required for immunity.

A combination of Vitamins B1 - B12 and B6 can be found in most breakfast cereals and also in lean meat, wholegrains, nuts, fish, orange juice, yeast extract, low-fat dairy produce and pulses.

Vitamin C helps the immune system and can be found in citrus fruits such as oranges, grapefruit also mangos, kiwi fruit and another good source is blueberries.

Blueberries are one of the best sources of immune boosting and can also help to fight cancer plus anti-aging antioxidants, so you can either buy them fresh or dry and ready-to-eat. Vitamin C is classed as the stress vitamin, and our daily requirement can vary quite a bit depending on emotions or other stress forms.

When you have heavy colds or flu, Vitamin C is useful to take daily and as it is water-soluble, ensure that you do take it daily.

Blueberry Smoothie recipe

Ingredients
175ml/6fl oz apple or orange juice
120ml/4fl oz natural yoghurt
1 banana, peeled and roughly chopped
170g/6oz blueberries (defrosted if frozen)

Preparation method
Place all the ingredients into a blender and blend until smooth.

To serve, pour into glasses

The mineral Zinc can be found in brazil nuts, pumpkin seeds, ginger, wholegrain, eggs, soy products and lean meat. A deficiency of zinc can compromise immunity, and there is really no need to take any supplements as there should be more than enough found in the foods listed above. Zinc is essential for growth and development, wound healing, insulin production, hair growth, skin, immunity, smell and taste.

Iron can be found in most green vegetables such as spinach and broccoli and the best source is the darker, leafy green vegetables, also liver, kidney and egg yolk.

Some other sources of iron are in dried beans, dried fruit such as raisins, figs and prunes. Iron is essential for the formation of haemoglobin of red blood cells. An iron-deficient condition is anaemia which can lead to being breathless and constantly tired.

Pause and take a mental time-out, then breathe - take a few deep breaths - in through your mouth and slowly out through your nose to release mounting tension. Relax and be more focused

What steps will you take now?

1 _____

2 _____

3 _____

4 _____

5 _____

6 _____

7 _____

8 _____

9 _____

10 _____

Part Three – Tried and Tested Ways to Help

10

Ways to Energise and Prevent Fatigue

There are many ways you can boost your immune system and it is vital that you strive to keep it healthy as much of the time as possible. Here are some suggestions which will help to boost your immune system and keep it healthy. Remember a healthy immune system improves your health and wellbeing and give your more energy, preventing fatigue.

Brown bread – if you like white bread, try brown bread with wholegrain as it contains protein, B vitamins, fibre and lots of nutrients.

Tofu or soya beans
It is low in fat, low in saturated fats and low in carbohydrates. Tofu is also rich in protein and contains all eight essential amino acids. Tofu is cholesterol-free and is low in sodium/salt which can help to reduce blood pressure, and it is also good as a natural alternative to HRT.

Green Tea

This is a very good source for important antioxidants and boosting the immune system. Any cup of tea will help the immune system as you are relaxing (or you should be) and try putting your feet up on a stool as you drink your tea slowly.

Beetroot

It is good either cooked or raw and is rich in iron which encourages the production of disease-fighting antibodies.

Garlic

This simple plant is at the top of every immune system enhancing list. Garlic also has general immune system boosting qualities, including antioxidant benefits. It is best to use fresh or at the end of cooking.

Yoghurt

Especially probiotic yoghurts which have good bacteria, and this can help to protect the body against harmful bacteria and infections. These are very important to ensure that the digestion system is working efficiently and effectively, so that you can absorb the nutrients from other foods which are essential for your immune system health.

Mushrooms

Mushrooms are immune enhancing and the best type is shiitake mushrooms, also maitake, oyster, and enokitake. Maitake mushrooms are high in nutrients including Vitamins B-2, C, D, niacin, magnesium, potassium, fibre, and amino acids, Maitake mushrooms contain polysaccharide compound beta-1.6-glucan and this naturally stimulates the immune system and lowers blood pressure. It is very useful for those who are obese or diabetic, and the maitake mushroom could be best known for its cancer fighting ability.

Shitake Mushrooms help to lower cholesterol and improves the immune system functioning and prevents high blood pressure and heart disease. They are good for controlling cholesterol levels, building resistance against viruses, and fighting diseases such as AIDS/HIV and cancers.

Dr. Shoji Shibata, a professor at Tokyo University conducted a study of well-known cancer-fighting and immune-boosting mushrooms which were compared to the ABM Mushroom (Agaricus Blazei Murrill) which is found in Brazil and included Reishi and Shitake. Dr. Shibata's results found that the other mushrooms were not as effective as the ABM mushroom, and so the ABM is at the top of the list of potent mushrooms which befits its other name, the "Mushroom of God"! There have been other Japanese and British studies which have also shown the ABM mushroom to have the highest concentration of beta-glucan of any mushroom. Beta Glucan is a powerful immune-enhancing nutritional supplement and it has a unique compound which is able to help the body defend itself against viral and bacterial invaders.

Broccoli

This is one of the top foods to boost the immune system. It contains significant levels of Vitamin A, Vitamin C, Vitamin E, and beta carotene; most of the top immune system nutrients.

Tuna

Contains many important nutrients for immune system health, and this includes selenium and omega-3 fatty acids, and an amount of zinc, while being very low in fats.

Oats

Oats are high in immunity-boosting Vitamin E as they break down cholesterol build-up which is thought to be able to help in the prevention of cancer. They also are rich in an anti-inflammatory mineral.

Sweet Potatoes

Sweet potatoes contain Vitamin A and have antioxidant properties which help to fight cancer. The potato skins are full of fibre and they can help to reduce cholesterol and also enhances the digestive system.

It is essential that you take some time out specifically for you and do not feel guilty about it. Having some 'me time' is essential so that you can have time to yourself at least once a week and you will feel so much better after it.

Drink less alcohol

When you are under stress, a few glasses of wine in the evening can help you relax and fall asleep. However, you sleep less deeply after drinking alcohol and the following day can leave you feeling tired even although you may have had 7-8 hours' sleep.

It helps if you can reduce alcohol intake before bedtime. This will result in a good night's sleep and rest resulting in having more energy.

Recommended alcohol intake should be: -

Men and women should ideally drink no more than 14 units a week regularly.

This is equivalent to six pints of average strength beer or six 175 ml glasses of low strength wine.

Drinking Water for More Energy

You may feel tired as you are feeling tired and this can be due to being slightly dehydrated. All you need is to drink a glass of water which will work effectively and even better after exercise.

Losing Weight Can Result in more Energy

When your body is carrying excess weight, it can be exhausting for you. It can put extra strain on your heart, which results in you feeling tired.

If you can lose some weight, this will make you feel more energetic. As well as eating healthily, the best way to lose weight is to be more active and have a regular exercise routine.

Beat tiredness by Eating often

To keep up your energy throughout the day, it is good if you can eat regular meals as well as healthy snacks about every three to four hours, rather than one large meal.

11

It is Time to be Positive and Happier

Staying Positive

Trying to look on the bright side is not always easy when you are busy, but it does help the immune system. Do you have a half full glass or a half empty glass? Hopefully, you have a half full one as our thoughts and feelings can impact on our immune system.

Being positive helps your overall outlook in life and even when things are not going well, there is always a small way that you can aim to be positive. Say to yourself that you will not be negative by saying you are unable to do something because of all the various excuses you may have. Take a step back and thin how you can turn those excuses into saying you can and will do this in a positive and enthusiastic way.

When you think you can't manage something, say to yourself

> "yes, I will try and see how I get on, and in time will get it perfected".

The more you say and try this, the more positive you will become. With being positive, it is practicing repeatedly as it is a skill that can be learnt. Have a coloured dot or something you can place where you can see it regularly to remind you to continue to be positive.

You can buy the coloured dots in stationery shops. I give these out at training classes and some people put it on their purse or wallet or name badge. It is best to change the dot from time to time to another colour as you soon get used to a colour and may not notice it.

Have a go at the Be Positive Activity at Chapter 15.

Laughter

Research has shown that laughter can be good for your health; laughter helps to reduce stress, stimulates digestion, reduce muscular tension and lower blood pressure. A really good laugh does help you forget your worries and does give a feel-good feeling even if it is for a short while. Try and see how you react.

What does make you laugh? Some research has shown that it is possible just to laugh and not at anything funny which could be quite hard to do, but it does work so try it and see. Keep laughing until you feel good about yourself and life in general.

Lifestyle

A lot of people would like a more holistic approach to life and don't want to be taking tranquillisers, anti-depressants and sleeping tablets. A more holistic approach could be aromatherapy, reflexology and other therapies.

To help the body, ensure the mind is more in tune with the body will result in a more relaxed lifestyle. If you sit on your hand and forget about it, over a few minutes it will become numb and you can become aware of it; this is trying to get your mind and body in tune with each other. Not so easy to do, but practice and try.

Many times, I am driving along the road and find that the car in front has their window wipers on even although the rain has stopped 5-10 minutes previously. I do wonder if the driver is concentrating on driving or in 'auto-pilot'. The mind and body are certainly not in tune!

Albert Einstein's formula for happiness was: -

> "A calm and humble life will bring more happiness than the pursuit of success and the constant restlessness that comes with it."

I was recently on an Air France flight from Johannesburg to Paris which was amazing. From the minute we stepped on the plane, we were greeted by happy and smiling flight attendants. This continued throughout the flight even although it was an overnight flight. On one occasion when I was waiting at the toilet I was again greeted by a happy, smiling flight attendant (not sure about the time as I don't check my watch or clock at night) but chatting as if it was daytime. It was like a breath of fresh air. Before we landed at Paris, 'our flight attendant' came around and said, 'au revoir' and wished us a pleasant day. This has never happened before on a flight no matter where in the world.

This was a great end to a fantastic holiday and I do wish this could happen more often. They obviously all worked well as a team and were happy at their job. In turn, their passengers were happy and content.

I will not mention about the outward flight!

Life is short, and no one has tomorrow guaranteed, so aim to be happy even although you do not feel like it. This is certainly one way to make you look and feel younger as you relax and release all the tension in your body and aim to not be worrying so much.

> *"Think of all the beauty that's still left in and around you, and be happy"*
> *~Anne Frank*

Your lifestyle can improve with small changes. Write down your current lifestyle and how you can improve it. There are some examples to get you started.

Current Lifestyle	Improved Lifestyle
Friends are great for social interaction and to be able to talk and share feelings when time allows.	
Our home is where we feel relaxed and comfortable or is it becoming the place you do not want to be living in?	

Current Lifestyle	Improved Lifestyle
No time to myself	Become more creative and active by swimming, golf, music or joining a painting group or try writing for a journal.

Remember – you are in control to improve
your lifestyle.

Start today and write down some actions.

12

Being Relaxed is Key to the Mind and Body being in Tune

Background to Relaxation training

Relaxation is defined by Ryman as 'a state of consciousness characterised by feelings of peace, and release from tension, anxiety and fear'. This emphasises the psychological part of relaxation, e.g. pleasant sensation and absence of stressful or unpleasant thoughts. The word 'relaxed' refers to lax muscles or to peaceful thoughts.

When the mind is relaxed, certain neurotransmitters called endorphins are released into the bloodstream from the brain and these can change the rhythms of the body. This helps to balance pressure in the body and alleviate stress.

Relaxation has three aims:

1. A preventive measure, to protect body organs from unnecessary wear and tear especially the organs involved in stress-related disease
2. As a treatment to help relieve stress in conditions such as tension headache, insomnia, asthma, immune deficiency, and panic.

3. As a coping skill to help calm the mind and allow clearer, more effective and efficient thinking.

Why Learn Relaxation?

With the pace of life nowadays, many of us do not have the time or even the energy to relax properly. You may have found that you could have unmanageable tension and that you need some help and assistance and the best option is training in the art of relaxation.

Once you learn how to relax by learning new techniques and skills, they can be used by you at anytime and anywhere at no additional cost. By using relaxation techniques when you have a demanding job or lifestyle will ensure that you remain alert and avoid fatigue. Do you feel some tension in your arms, shoulders, back of the neck or your head? This is a build-up of tension and if left, could become chronic.

Physical effects of muscular tension are:-
  - Tension headaches
  - Eye strain
  - Migraine
  - Neck ache, Back ache
  - Palpitations
  - Stomach cramps
  - Exhaustion
  -

Getting Started

Make sure you find time, a suitable quiet place, and that you are comfortable either lying down or on a comfortable chair. Think about having some background music, no interruptions, and don't feel guilty if you are 'sitting doing nothing' as what you are doing is very important for you and those round about you. Try not to relax soon after eating as this can cause indigestion. It is more beneficial if you practice relaxation about 2 hours after a meal.

Benefits of Relaxation

Relaxation can be learnt by anyone and can be built into your everyday life.   It involves no drugs, difficult exercises and once learnt costs you nothing.

Advantages in practicing relaxation are that it can:

- Reduce the stress response
- Reduce pain, muscle tension, aches and pains
- Reduce fatigue
- Promotes sleep and allows the body to rest peacefully with a calm mind.
- Improve personal relationships and become more relaxed
- Increase self-esteem through self-awareness
- Look and feel younger

Activity - How do you relax?

Make a list of the ways, good and bad, you currently relax.

1.

2.

3.

4.

5.

6.

Learn new skills to relax

With the pace of life nowadays, there are computers, smart and mobile phones to the extent that no one has any time to set aside and relax properly. When we go out in the car everyone is in a rush and trying to pass either on the outside lane or if they can't manage that then they try to pass on the inside lane, and it doesn't seem to matter to them either that they are in 30 or 40 miles per hour zone.

It is amazing the amount of people who have unmanageable tension within their bodies and their shoulders and neck, to the extent that they are constantly trying to lower their shoulders as they are 'creeping up' towards their ears. If this happens to you on a regular basis, then try some of the relaxation techniques in this book because once you have learnt them you can practice them anywhere and at any time. This will lead to you feeling a lot better with little or no tension in your body.

Everyone does need to learn how to relax and it should be part of our daily lives, but somehow just don't seem able to. By using relaxation techniques on a regular basis can lead to a much more pleasant and less stressful lifestyle.

Relaxation can be learnt by anyone and it can be built into your everyday life to the point that you won't need to think about it and can almost do it automatically.

The advantages to learning relaxation are the reduction of pain especially due to muscle tension, and various aches and pains. It is also ideal as a treatment which can help relieve stress especially if you suffer from tension headaches, insomnia, panic attacks and immune deficiency.

Relaxation can help to calm the mind and helps you to think much more clearly.

Relationship between Stress and Relaxation

When you are feeling Stressed	Symptoms	When you are Relaxed
↑	Heart rate	↓
↑	Respiratory rate	↓
↑	Blood pressure	↓

↑	Muscle tension	↓
↑	Adrenaline	↓
↑	Sweating	↓

From the above it is clear to see how the body responds to relaxation, and when relaxing on a regular basis, you will see most of the changes being virtually opposite to those induced by the stress response. Is this not a good reason to be relaxing more often? There are various CDs or you can download music onto a MP3 player, iPod, your computer or a mobile phone.

A reduction in feeling tired all the time is helped by relaxing before going to sleep which will in turn promote sleep and allows your body to rest more peacefully with a calmer mind. You will feel much better in the morning and this will give you a boost to start the day well and be more positive about life in general.

Your personal relationships will be much improved because you are and feel more relaxed. It can also help to increase your self-esteem, and this is through self-awareness of how you are acting and reacting to various situations. This is learnt over a period of time by identifying what does cause you to become tense and stressed.

Would you like to relax just now?

- Close your eyes
- Sit up straight in your chair
- Pull your shoulders down, and then let them go
- Move your jaw from side to side
- Shake your hands down by your side
- Place palms upwards on your lap
- Breathe in and out slowly
- Let your legs flop and relax

Sit for about 5-10 minutes and note how you feel at the end of the short relaxation.

One of the first things to learn about relaxation is to learn to relax both your body and mind and it is a case of re-educating ourselves. How this is done is to be able to tune in our mind and body to each other. This may at first sound a bit funny, but an example is if you are sitting on a chair and you sit on your hand without realising what you are actually doing.

After a short time, it starts to feel numb and you then become aware of it; during that period of time, where was your mind and body? Another example can be seen on a regular basis, when you are in the car you may see a driver in front of you with their window wipers on and the rain has been off for the past ten minutes. Are their mind and body functioning as 'one'? In situations like this it demonstrates that the mind is away somewhere else thinking of many other things and not concentrating on the job in hand – driving!

Try to relax properly before you sleep, and this will lead to slower breathing which will result in less oxygen being required. Your metabolic activity gradually slows down when you are asleep, and you will find that both your hand and foot temperatures should increase when relaxed.

Sleep

Sleep is what comes naturally to us from birth and will help to balance and give us more energy. No one needs any training in this form of relaxation, as our bodies will naturally let us know when certain functions need to recharge. It is important that we take note of 'what our bodies are saying to us'.

When we are feeling tired, then it is time to rest and sleep rather than trying to fight it. We spend almost one third of our lives asleep which is an amazing amount of time. When you are deprived of sleep for a few days, it has been found that people can start to show signs of mental instability and physical frustration.

Research has shown that people who have not had any sleep may hallucinate. When we are asleep, we are totally relaxed, and neuro-chemicals are released from the brain which helps to recharge and rebuild our body functions. It is this natural process of falling asleep which is so vital to receiving the great benefits of a good night's sleep.

When you take drugs to help you sleep, such as herbal remedies or prescribed drugs, it does create a false method of relaxation and it may not be relaxing at all, since the slow method of falling into a deep state of relaxation does not occur at all. This is when the practice of relaxation techniques comes in to being as between the two worlds of wakefulness and sleep. When we are unable to fall asleep naturally, this can be due to an excessive build-up of tension, which can prevent the natural sleep process from occurring. It really does mean that you need to re-educate both the body and mind for a more positive and effective approach to having a good night's sleep every single night.

Before going to bed at night, it is good to practice relaxation techniques between being awake and falling asleep, and it really does mean that you need to re-educate the mind and body. Once practiced, it can be carried out time and time again effectively.

If you wake up during the night and cannot get back to sleep because you are worried, then have a notepad and pen beside your bed, so that you can jot any worries down. Once you have written down all that is causing you concern, you will feel relieved and as a result fall asleep.

Tips for Relaxation

For relaxation to be effective you need to set some time aside as well as a quiet room or space and either a comfortable chair or bed or the floor. Have some relaxing, soothing music on in the background only if this is what suits you and make sure that no one is going to interrupt you.

> *Relaxation should be carried out at least two hours after a meal otherwise you cannot relax properly with a full stomach.*

See if you can build some daily relaxation techniques into your life, even diary it in and put it in your calendar on your mobile phone, tablet, pc or calendar. When you are more relaxed, you can become more self-confident, self-aware, and motivated. Relaxation is not compatible with worry, anxiety and tension, so that is a good enough reason to build relaxation into your daily routine. So how about getting started NOW!

Progressive Relaxation

This is ideal to help you to relax and very useful prior to going to sleep. It is a slightly abbreviated version and you can tailor it to what suits you. Remember to start at the top, your eyes, and then work down your body to your toes, tensing and releasing.

Progressive Relaxation – you could record this and play back on your phone or pc or whatever is best for you

1. Loosen any tight clothing around neck or waist area. Remove eye glasses.

2. Lie flat on your back, pillow under your head, and support under your knees.

3. Legs slightly apart, rolled out from the hips and feet falling outwards.

4. Try to practice this position.

5. Feel the contact with the chair, floor, or bed through your back, legs, thighs, buttocks, head, shoulders and arms.

6. Concentrate on your breathing and count 3 breaths in and then 3 breaths out. Encourage

deep breathing into your abdomen which helps to control stress. Place your hands on your abdomen and as you breathe in your abdomen should rise. Practice this a few times.

7. As you breathe out feel the tension being released throughout your body and give a few deep sighs to "let go".

8. Relax your mind and think of something pleasant and focus on that or listen to your breathing or listen to the background music.

9. You are now ready for progressive relaxation.

10. Curl your toes and hold tight for about a minute feeling the tension and then slowly release.

11. Tighten your calf muscles, hold tight for about a minute feeling the tension and then slowly release.

12. Now tighten your buttocks, hold tight for about a minute feeling the tension and then slowly release.

13. Tighten your abdomen, hold tight for about a minute feeling the tension and then slowly release.

14. Now clench your hands, making a fist hold tight for about a minute feeling the tension and then slowly release.

15. Raise your shoulders right up towards your ears hold tight for about a minute feeling the tension and then slowly release.

16. Move your head gently from side to side.

17. Yawn and clench your teeth hold tight for about a minute feeling the tension and then slowly release.

18. Now screw up your eyes hold tight for about a minute feeling the tension and then slowly release.

19. Frown hold tight for about a minute feeling the tension and then slowly release.

20. You are now feeling totally relaxed and warm.

21. Visualise something pleasant, maybe the beach when you were on holiday or somewhere you like to walk. Visualise yourself at that place and if any thoughts stray in, forget about them and go back to your special place and visualise.

22. 10-minute relaxation.

23. Now bring tension back into your life, be aware of your surroundings, the chair, the bed or floor. Wriggle your toes, wriggle your fingers, then stretch your arms and then stretch your legs. Ease your back, ease your shoulders, move your head and then open your eyes.

24. When you are ready, turn onto your side first and then very slowly sit up.

This relaxation can be part of your weekly routine and it could be carried out when everyone is out of the house and you have some time to yourself. It can be just before you go to sleep and once you have learnt how to carry it out, you can tailor it to what suits you and when. You will soon get used to feeling tension within your body and what you should be doing to prevent it.

After the activity, how did you feel?   ☺

Activity – Relaxation

Have a think about ways you are going to relax.

1.

2.

3.

4.

5.

13

Using Your Senses Will Energise You

When we become aware of our senses it is a form of mindfulness by seeing, hearing, feeling, tasting and touching enables us to be more relaxed and less stressed. Take your time and be mindful.

I attended mindfulness classes a few years ago so that I would be able to explain about them when I was running training sessions and coaching. One of the things I remember was the tutor explaining about taking a shower in the morning. First you listen to the water falling onto your skin and then onto the shower base, feel the water on your skin whether it is hot, cold or warm, smell the soap or shower gel and take your time whilst you shower. See how you get on the next time you shower or have a bath and take your time and be mindful.

I was coaching a client called Ian, who was under a lot of stress due to major issues at work. I explained to him when he went out into the fresh air, even for a short while, to breathe in the fresh air with slow breaths in and to breathe slowly out, listen to the birds and look at them in the sky, listen to any other noises in the background or maybe it is peaceful, be aware of the temperature and how you feel. If he was eating, I suggested that he take time tasting it and chewing slowly and this also helps digestion as well as being relaxing.

The next coaching session, Ian reported that he found the experience very relaxing and made him appreciate what was going on round about it and helped him also to focus on improving his own mental wellbeing.

These are good methods to help you to relax as well as to focus in that moment.

Sense of smell

Our sense of smell can instinctively cause us to feel happy or in fear; this could be the smell of flowers which can make you feel happy and content, or if you smell fire it could mean that you need to run for your life, depending on the situation.

For symptoms such as anxiety, insomnia and aggression, there are some essential oils which are ideal to help you to relax and these are camomile, lavender, vanilla, rose and neroli essential oils.

A few drops can be used in your bath or a few drops can be added to a tea light candle before you light it. **Add the oil prior to lighting the candle.** Depending on how strong you like it will depend on how much to use, however, start with a couple of drops and decide if you would like more or are happy as it is.

A favourite essential oil is lavender and is possibly the best one for relaxation. It does help you to relax, and at the same time, it also eases aches and pains, such as headaches. You can sprinkle four drops on a tissue and inhale deeply for sudden stress.

Lavender Spritzer

Add a few drops of lavender oil to 50mls of distilled water and this can be put in 50ml spray bottles which are available from pharmacies or shops.

The spray lasts ages and is always lovely and fresh. It can be sprayed over your pillow before going to bed and you could keep one in the hall which is handy especially when you are expecting visitors, or you just want a fresh and uplifting fragrance.

Sandalwood and nutmeg can also help to relieve some of the effects of stress, and they could also be used along with other techniques.

Patchouli oil can lift your mood, and some say that it is also an aphrodisiac.

There are some Essential Oils which have been found to useful for worry and managing stress.

Calming Oils	Uplifting Oils	Stress Oils	Oils to avoid if pregnant
Cedarwood Chamomile Geranium Lavender	Basil Bergamot Geranium Juniper	Chamomile Geranium Lavender Marjoram	Basil Bay Comfrey Hyssop

Marjoram Melissa Neroli Rose Sandalwood Vanilla Ylang Ylang	Lavender Melissa	Melissa Peppermint Sandalwood	Juniper Marjoram Melissa Sage

Essential Oil Blends

There are some essential oil combinations which are good if you wish to relax and feel a bit calmer. Try different combinations and then you will find which one is best for you, but it would be advisable to ask at health shops or a holistic therapist. It is best not to mix more than three oils unless someone has recommended doing so.

Relaxing Blend
The following blend can be used in a vaporiser or in a bath.

2 drops geranium
2 drops lavender
2 drops sandalwood
1 drop ylang-ylang

Blends can be purchased from various shops, health food shops or pharmacies.

When under stress, you may suffer from low self-esteem as well as lacking in self-confidence, which is really frustrating especially when trying to get services organised and the appropriate support required. There are some essential oils which are good for that extra boost; these are jasmine, rose and grapefruit essential oils. Check out the section on self-esteem and self-confidence.

Touch

Touching someone can help such as placing your hand on their shoulder to give some encouragement and to let them know that you support and acknowledge them. Touch is a form of communication and can make you feel valued and more aware of your body. It is amazing what the sense of touch can do and makes you feel warm and supported, as well as realising that others do understand what you are actually going through at that period of time. Of course, it can also depend who puts their hand on your shoulder and it could have the opposite affect!

Hands on therapy such as massage therapies can be very helpful for some people and a massage can be very relaxing, however the effects of a massage can last for a day or two.

Massage can have a calming effect on the nervous system which will give a feeling of wellbeing and takes away tension. A massage will help to slow down your heart rate plus lowering blood pressure. So why not treat yourself or at least try one. There are lots of different therapies that may be available within your local area. Some examples are:

Aromatherapy

Aromatherapy is a holistic treatment and is defined as the art and science of utilising naturally extracted essences from plants to balance, harmonise and promote the health of body and mind. It is a healing art and uses essential oils and massage ensuring that both smell and touch senses are being used effectively.

Some of the key benefits of Aromatherapy are:

- Physical
- Psychological
- Improves muscular pain
- Anxiety
- Mild depression
- Grieving process
- Improves the immune system
- Menopausal symptoms and PMS
- Respiratory complaints such as coughs, tonsillitis, and sinusitis

Reflexology

There are two different types of reflexology and they are hands or feet. Reflexology is based on the principle that reflex points on the feet are connected to corresponding areas throughout the body. The feet can be seen as a 'map' of the body and the organs of the body are mirrored in the feet. This is by applying pressure to certain points which relates to a zone of the body, an example is the lower back which relates to the heel. When a Reflexologist presses on the feet in a certain way, this could identify where there may be a problem with a particular organ.

Reflexology is the term that describes a form of massage, usually applied either to the feet or hands, which has a beneficial effect on health because its effect is to:

- Improve the circulation of blood and lymph
- Increase the supply of oxygen and nutrients
- to tissues
- Helps to remove waste from tissues
- Promotion of deep relaxation

No matter what the initial presenting condition is, the effect is to stimulate the body to achieve its own point of balance, and this can have a beneficial effect not only on the physical body, but also on the mind. The method is to work on the reflexes with thumbs and fingers as in specialised massage techniques, said to help correct imbalances throughout the body and release blocked qi (energy).

Hand Reflexology is the same as 'foot' reflexology, with the reflex points found on the hands instead of the feet. There are some therapists who may work on corresponding reflex points on the hands and feet simultaneously to enhance treatment.

Some of the key benefits of reflexology are:-

- Emotional and psychological benefits
- Relieves stress
- Promotion of calm and well being
- Helps insomnia
- Relieves fatigue
- Helps relieve muscular tension

Jessica M Smyrl

Relaxation Therapy

Relaxation Therapy includes techniques that can effectively reduce stress and triggers the body's relaxation response. The techniques are easy to do, fun and relaxing, and can be used by anyone who wishes to help manage stress and worry. Relaxation Therapy promotes wellness and healing, it also serves as a great complementary therapy for those recovering from illness and guided imagery is one technique frequently used for healing.

Some of the key benefits of relaxation therapy are:-

- Relieves Muscle Tension
- Reduces Pain
- Reduces worry
- Reduces insomnia and fatigue by deep, sound sleep
- Reduces stomach problems by helping digestion
- Increases concentration, memory and a clearer focus
- Increases Self-Confidence and Self-esteem
- Increases Energy and Productivity
- Helps the Immune System to be healthier

Yoga

Yoga is a 'complete science of life' as physical exercises, known as 'asanas', are practised on a regular basis will help to strengthen and tone the nervous system, relieve tension, improve circulation and increase flexibility. Each asana is based on a stretch, when the body is held still for a period of time until the hold has been achieved, and this is whilst the mind is concentrating, and relaxing the body, so is also able to breathe deeper and more rhythmic, and these all help to maintain each hold.

The word 'Yoga' comes from the ancient Asian language called Sanskrit and it is a name as well as a way of life that means 'union, 'inner harmony', or 'peace'. It has become more popular over the past forty years.

Laughter Yoga or Hasyayoga

This is a form of yoga which is self-triggered laughter. The laughter is physical in nature and does not necessarily involve humour or comedy and it is becoming more popular as an exercise routine.

Laughter Yoga is a revolutionary idea – simple and profound. It is an exercise routine and is a complete wellbeing workout. Laughter Yoga is based on a scientific fact that our bodies cannot tell the difference between false and real laughter. They both have the same physiological and psychological benefits.

Hatha Yoga is the type of yoga which is the most frequently used in Western countries and it seeks union, wholeness and harmony for the whole being through physical exercise. It concentrates on the whole person and helps to relax certain muscle groups, develop and improve body circulation and improves well-being.

Some of the key benefits of Yoga are:

- A relaxed body and tranquil mind
- Vitality
- Improved breath control

- Improved health
- Suppleness
- Weight control
- Youthfulness
- Better mental performance
- Improved emotional stability

14

Be more Productive, Happier and Healthier

How many hours of sleep do you normally get? Ideally, you should try for about eight hours per night and often the best way to get to sleep each night is to try and get into a routine. You may not be sleeping well due to worries and this is happening on a regular basis. Have a word with your manager as you should be able to work flexible working hours if that would be an option for you, even for a short period of time. Some options could be working from home or going in earlier or later during the working day, as long as you work your contracted hours. You may wish to reduce your hours for a short time until you feel well enough.

Body and mind awareness helps towards a healthier lifestyle

Learning to relax the body and mind is a means of re-educating ourselves. We tend to forget the feelings within the body and go in the direction of the mind e.g. twisting our necks, sitting on our hand. This does mean being out of touch with our bodies balance and requirements and is one of the main causes of stress. If you practice relaxation, this helps both body and mind by becoming more self-aware.

To help reduce worries and reduce pain perception – think of a nature scene, such as a meadow, forest, beach or a scene you can think of and can relax. Try out a relaxation technique such as tense-release and feel the tension and anxiety flow away. There are some techniques in the chapter with Activities.

Visualisation Therapy/Technique

Visualisation or imagery is a technique where the mind is stimulated to think of visual images of nice, pleasant and positive objects or scenes. Imagery is excellent to control the stress response and it can help to reduce and control mental anxiety by visualising pleasant, relaxing images and thoughts.

Over the years, research has shown that we can mentally picture our bodies doing something and internal changes can occur as well.

An example is could be imagining you are walking along the beach in the sun, and this can cause our muscles to tense as we run and our brain waves will alter which can result in our sweat glands becoming more active. It has been shown with biofeedback research that if we are to imagine pleasant warm scenes in the sun, we can actually feel warmth through all parts of our body.

If you are having difficulty in visualising a relaxing scene, look for a picture or a post card and imagine that you are lying on a beach or sitting or walking on a mountainside enjoying the fresh open spaces. Then close your eyes and concentrate on that scene whilst you relax. If your mind starts to think of other thoughts, go back to the pleasant scene and enjoy the relaxation.

Try some of the relaxation techniques or just slow down or sit in a comfortable chair and breathe in deeply, in through your nose and slowly out through your mouth. Slow down your breathing and keep your thoughts on the relaxing scene for 10-15 minutes.

Some of the key benefits of Visualisation Therapy are:
- Reduces worries
- Improves immune system
- Relaxed body and mind
- Assists competitiveness when performing in sports
- Become more positive

When you are in a Stressful Situation

You will probably have to attend meetings at work which can be a stressful situation and it is best to be well-prepared so that you don't forget to say something important and remember an hour or two later.

Try and visualise the meeting and rehearse various scenarios through imagery of what will be said and reactions of others and yourself. Take yourself through the door and then walking into the meeting and seeing all the people sitting there. Make sure you see yourself smiling as you sit down, being positive, upbeat, calm and most importantly relaxed with a good posture. If you are able to visualise the situation beforehand, you will find that you are well prepared, and this will ensure that all will go well. You can try this a few times until you feel calmer and controlled. Jot down all the points you wish to raise before you go into the meeting and this will help you feel more focused.

Characteristics of
On-the-Spot Techniques

Lichstein (1988) described the main points of these techniques as: -

- Portable: short enough and convenient enough to be used in most situations
- Unobtrusive: not attracting attention or interrupting ongoing work
- Capable of inducing moderate levels of relaxation. The object is not to induce deep relaxation but to enable the individual to carry on with the task, in as relaxed a state as possible.

Shake a sleeve down

This is a very quick technique and all you require to do is to stand up and shake your arm down as if you are trying to bring the sleeve down to your wrist. Do this a few times and feel the muscles in the arm and shoulder loosening. Try this any time you are feeling tense.

Posture

How many times are you out or you see others when you are out and about who are slouching as they are walking and dragging their heels, looking as if the weight of the world is on them and looking miserable. If this is you, then stop, change and to boost your confidence and well-being, 'think tall', and 'think up' so when you are out you will feel much better and you will also be able to smile at others as you become more confident. This is a quick and easy method to remember and the benefits are well worth it.

'Me time'

Make sure you set aside some time for yourself at least once a week and this is so that you can take a step back and recharge your batteries. This could be going out with friends or reading a book or something that you like and enjoy doing. How about having a long soak in the bath? Make a note of it in your diary so that you will not forget!

Self-talk

This is extremely powerful, and you find that prominent statesmen and singers do this before they go on stage. Effective self-talk can be phrases such as:

- 'I can't manage', 'I always lose', 'I just can't cope'.
- You could change to 'yes, it is okay to be a bit anxious; I know what I should and can do'

- Afterwards say 'I may have been a bit anxious, but less than before'

The more you say these words to yourself, the more you can and will achieve. Always give yourself a positive thought at the end to say that you have done well, and then the next time you can do even better and so on.

Feel Great About Yourself

The first time I heard about self-talk was when I was having coaching sessions before an interview for my own job. The coach was a sports coach and he had a day job as an accountant and sports coach in the evenings.

He would come to my home one evening a week and I would get homework from him. On one evening, I was given the task of saying that I feel great. I was to repeat 'I feel great' all the way to work the next morning. I said that I didn't feel great, but it is the power of self-talk that repeating it repeatedly will make you feel and believe that you are.

The next morning as I drove to work I kept repeating the phrase, I parked the car and then went up three flights of stairs and by the time I had reached the third floor, I walked along the corridor as if I was walking on air, feeling great and no one was going to change that feeling. The first person I say was a colleague who was very serious and ask how I was when I said, 'I am great' he looked at me as if I was not feeling myself. Anyway, I kept saying it all day and continued to feel great. To this day, I still say it at training sessions and often say it to myself even although I may not feel it. I know it does work, but it is to practice, practice, practice the skills and believe it and no one will make you feel otherwise.

Let no one make you feel any different to the way you do feel, unless of course you let them. Remember the phrase "sticks and stones may break my bones, but words can never hurt me".

Small Bite-sized chunks

If the job or task is too much, divide into small bite-sized chunks which you can handle and ignore what you can't do at that time. Try and focus on one task or goal, one by one. A good way to deal with this is to write down a list of all the tasks you have, then prioritise and once you have done this, then fold the paper into say six pieces and cut them, so you can see and deal with one at a time.

Once you have tried this, you can make this part of your routine as it is a good way to manage tasks which could be causing you to become very stressed about. Give yourself a treat when you achieve each task.

Reduce Stress with Coloured Markers

Reduce stress markers are all different coloured dots which can be stuck on something which is a potential source of stress. Each time you see the marker, it will remind you that you require maintaining low levels of stress.

A stress marker is a coloured dot which can be stuck on something that is causing you to become stressed. An example could be appliances which are potential sources of stress, e.g. the phone if it is always ringing and annoying you, then put on a stress marker to remind you to put the answering machine on if you are not in the right frame of mind or too busy to answer.

Another source could be when you are driving and feeling uptight or angry with other drivers or yourself, then put one on the steering wheel to remind you to maintain low levels of tension.

The stress markers require to be changed frequently as you soon become used to seeing a colour, so change it to another colour each time you feel it is necessary and this could be about every two weeks.

If it is an individual who is causing you to become stressed, write down their name and a marker beside it, or if you have a picture, place a marker on it.

15
___

How to Improve your Confidence and Self-esteem

Here are some ways which can help boost your confidence and self-esteem.

When you are under stress, you can very quickly lose your confidence and self-esteem. It can take time to boost yourself to get to the level you were before or even beyond that. Here are some ways which will help, and it is with practice that it will can help you.

Anticipate issues

Before going to bed, write down a few thoughts about your day, how you felt, your hopes and plan for the next day. This can be in a journal which can make you look back and see how far you have come. Put stress-relieving thoughts and any feelings that you have down as well as aspirations you may have.

You can look back at the journal and see the progress you have made and what you have achieved.

Blow your tension away

Breathe in noisily and exaggerate the effort, hold the breath for a slow count of 5, then very slowly blow away the tension in small puffs until all the tension has been blown away. Do this several times until you feel more relaxed.

Short breathing tip to relax

Try to slow your breathing down, so slowly breathe in through your nose and then slowly let that breath go out through your mouth to relax and stay calm. Continue to do this for a few minutes until you feel more relaxed. This can be done at any time and in any place and is especially good if you are going into a stressful situation such as speaking to your boss or a customer.

How to be Assertive Without Being Aggressive

Being assertiveness means that you are being clear about:

1. What you want
2. What your needs are
3. How you feel.

Sometimes it is a case of saying 'no' to yourself when you may have unrealistic expectations of yourself. The only person who will be affected will be you, as you will be so tired and then you can become angry resulting in getting annoyed with loved ones when you don't really mean to.

It is not so easy saying 'no' to others when you don't want to meet their request because you haven't got the time or want to do it or possibly feel unable to do it. You don't wish to hurt anyone's feelings, but you do at times need to think about yourself.

As human beings, we like to please others and do not like to offend, but there are times when you not only have to consider yourself but your close circle of friends and relatives. Weigh up the pros and cons of going out, for example, and if you don't want to, then on this occasion, say 'no' and you do not need to say the word 'no'.

An example could be "I would prefer to go another time when it is more suitable for me". There is no need to give an excuse, just leave it at that. People tend to respect you more for saying 'no' rather than agreeing with everyone and then you are labelled as 'oh B.....will always do that or will say ....'.

Practice and find effective and constructive ways of saying 'no' which takes time and practice, and you very rarely need to say 'no', there are other variations.

It is useful to be aware and ready when the other person is speaking to you and three points which I find useful are: -

1. Listen to what the other person is saying
2. Say what you are thinking and feeling
3. Say what you would like to happen

The other person is wanting you to go out this evening and you usually do but, on this occasion, you have something you need to do so here is what you could say.

An example could be:

"It would be good to go out this evening, but I need to prepare for tomorrow, so I need to do that".

Being assertive will most certainly help you with coping in life and being aware that you are important. There is a very thin line between being assertive and aggressive. However, when you are being aggressive, your body language gives you away by your facial expression and the way you stand. With assertiveness, it is practice that makes you manage to say 'no' without feeling that you are offending people and you will feel much better about yourself. This all helps to boost your confidence and improve your self-esteem.

Assertiveness Activity
The following are a few statements. Please read and think what you would say for each scenario. There is a space in between each scenario, so jot down your thoughts in pencil at first and then once you have read the whole book, you can come back to the activity and see if you still have the same thoughts.

1. You are asked to work late

2. You are in a shop and wanting to pay for some items, but the shop assistants are engrossed in a conversation. What will you do?

3. You are asked 'will you help me out'. You are always helping this friend out and it is never reciprocated so how will you say 'no' this time?

4. You are out at a coffee shop and you are given a seat right beside the toilets.

5. Someone goes in front of you in a queue at the supermarket. How will you deal with this?

6. You want to change your dental appointment from tomorrow.

How to handle people who are:

Aggressive
Dominant
Conflict
Criticism

Dealing with Aggression

When you are in a situation and find people, who do the following towards you such as finger pointing, leaning forward, sharp, sarcastic, fist thumping, loud voice, and shouting. What do you do?

You can say to them "will you please stop shouting" and they may not have realised that they were shouting and stop! On the other hand, they could continue shouting.

I had a situation when a man in the office building I was working in came into a room I had booked. He thought I hadn't and started shouting at me to get out of the room. He continued shouting even although I said several times to "stop shouting". I had to keep repeating myself and said that I would leave the room when I was ready. His face was bright red and I am sure that he would have been fuming for hours to come as possibly no one had ever spoken like that to him before. He was a bully and should not have got away with shouting at someone he didn't know. I have never seen him since thankfully but a very unpleasant individual.

Another option if you feel confident enough is to put your hand up and say, stop and walk away until they calm down and can talk to you in an appropriate and effective manner.

Dealing with Dominant People

- 'How can I be able to resist the pressure and dominance of excessively dominant people?'

- 'How can I stand up to bullies (or one bully in particular)?'

You require dealing in an assertive manner and you can often find that these people are being dominant for the sake of being dominant and this should not be seen as a natural behaviour for most people.

Dealing with conflict

The best thing to do is to resolve whatever the issue is, and this can be by listening to the other person's point of view and then try to negotiate and reach a compromise. Otherwise, whatever the issue is, it could get worse and could blow out of all proportion.
We all look at things in a different way and it could be that maybe one person is looking at it in one way and the other in a completely different way. It is a case to see which way is better or even try each way out and decide which works better. It is very much a bit of give and take and compromise.

Should it get worse, then mediation may be the answer.

Make a list of all the *successes* you have had. Start as far back as you can, and this can be exams, passing your driving test, speaking up for yourself. You will be surprised at how long the list will be and you could even start from several years ago.

Dealing with Criticism

The main thing to do is to keep away or avoid anyone who is criticising you as this can have a very negative effect on you. However, if someone does criticise you, stay calm and listen to what they have to say, and this should result in a win-win situation. You may say that you understand their criticism and take note of what they are saying.

Turn it round to a positive reaction "thank you for drawing it to my attention, but everyone else had the opposite remark to you and appreciated what I was doing". Usually these people don't want to hear this!

It is always better to listen to gratitude and praise, so remember to give it when it is justified. You feel better and the person receiving it feels good as well.

Confidence Diary

Start a diary or make it part of a journal, to say how confident you are feeling each day or on a weekly basis and over time, you will become more confident. You will not become confident overnight, but let it build up. Just being able to be confident and say exactly what you feel, without hurting others. This leads to better self-esteem, but it takes time and utilise your new skills to get to the level you are wanting to get to. Taking small steps is the way to get there.

Open Expression

An open expression will show that you mean what you say, and you are being quietly confident. By having this expression, gives others the opinion that you can be trusted.

Relaxed posture will help you feel more confident and level shoulders indicate and make you feel less tension within them. When they are up or hunched this can show that you are lacking in self-esteem. Good eye contact and a gentle smile as you speak or walk into a room is essential so try it out several times or in the mirror which is a great place to start as it can empower you.

Body language

Your face and your body should be 'saying the same things'. If you stand with arms outstretched saying that you are happy with what is being said, then anyone would accept that. However, if you were to stand with your arms folded and smiling, this would indicate that you could be hiding something.

There are examples on body language under the Communication Skills section of this chapter.

Value your own needs

Remember that you are important, and you need to realise that your needs are valuable to you. We all have needs. Assertiveness is not about your needs being met at the expense of others. It is about establishing everybody's needs and finding a course of action which reflects them all. This may involve compromise which is weighing up all the pros and cons and deciding what is the best course of action. Some negotiation may be required as you also require valuing others needs which need to be taken into consideration and each side should have or at least feel that they have equal positions.

Direct

Be direct when you are talking to others and say what your position is and here are some examples you can practice with: -

- 'I felt offended when you' as opposed to 'you were being rude when you...'
- 'I do not feel able to do all of this' as opposed to 'you expect too much of me'
- 'I am unclear what you want me to do here' as opposed to 'you keep changing what I should be doing'

Respectful

Be respectful to others and always let them give their opinion in their own time and then you give your opinion. This results in a positive response.

Share successes

So often we do not share successes, so give others and yourself a pat on the back when there are successes to celebrate. Make a list of all the successes you have had over the years and you will be surprised how many there are and keep adding to the list. Try out the activity earlier in this chapter.

Never assume

It is best to never assume because you like something, others will. Give them the opportunity to say how they feel.

Activity

Some examples for you to think about:

- Making a telephone call – the member of staff is always at meetings

- No one contacting you when you have left messages to return a call or get in touch. This happens time and time again. What would you do?

- Asking for help – would you?

- How to say no and not offend

- I can't do anymore!

What would you do in these circumstances now? Would your approach be different being a bit more assertive? If the answer is yes, then keep practicing so that when you need to be assertive, you can manage without even thinking about it.

Self-Confidence

When you are well prepared, this will increase your self-confidence and enable you to be assertive about what's important to you.

The way to build confidence is to apply positive thinking to performance, think positively, and have confident body language as well as good posture. Always concentrate on success and forget about not managing and move on quickly. The secret here is to always think of being a success at whatever you are doing and the saying "if at first you don't succeed, try, try and try again" is sometimes true and it does work.

Having a confident handshake says a lot about you. Make sure you don't have a handshake like a piece of fish – damp and floppy. Practice with someone else or even with both your hands by making sure you hold the other person's hand firmly as shown below.

Your thumb should go into the space between the other person's index finger and thumb – practice and you should get on well.

Summary – to be more assertive

- Express what your needs are and what your position is clearly
- Value yourself
- Communicate effectively
- Handle conflict openly and directly
- Negotiate
- Compromise
- Boosts your self-esteem and confidence

I Feel Great Notes:

Activity - Being Positive

When you have positive thoughts, it helps that you will also have positive feelings. Once you are able to say more often some positive statements, then you will both value yourself and will feel much better about yourself. Keep thinking positive thoughts and try to add to the following list. Your own phrases will let you become more relaxed about yourself and how you feel.

I feel calm

I do care

I am relaxed

I am in total control

I can do this

I am a great person

I feel great

I will manage to do this

I ....

I ....

I ....

I ....

I will be more positive by doing

_____

_____

_____

I was positive recently and will continue

_____

_____

_____

16
_____

How to Communicate More Effectively and be More Organised

There are different ways to communicate with each other and it is important to be able to say what you feel, what you are thinking about and what you want. How can anyone know what you are thinking, feeling or wanting? So, tell them in a pleasant way and this will make you feel a lot better. Write down a few bullet points before you go to a meeting or before you see someone, so you won't forget. This will help to boost your self-esteem and it is a case of patting yourself on the back to say, "yes I did it, and I did well by saying how I felt".

Amazingly, you will feel more energised and ready for the next time, so try it and see how you get on. It will also help to reduce any anger or aggression you may feel towards yourself or to others as it can build up to the point that you are almost 'boiling over'. The best way is to keep practicing and then it becomes part and parcel of being YOU.

Ronnie works as an Administrator and he was finding that one of his work colleagues was always assuming that he wanted to go for lunch first every day. Ronnie was getting fed up with this but did not want to say anything in case he upset his colleague and then there would be an atmosphere.

After discussing with him about a good course of action, Ronnie found enough courage to say to his colleague that he wanted to go later as he wasn't hungry, and it would be good if they could alternate times for lunch. His colleague agreed to this and Ronnie was shocked as he expected him to get very annoyed as he could be difficult at times. This left Ronnie feeling upbeat and energised.

The power of being positive and the way we think helps our overall mental attitude and with Ronnie it helped him greatly. He felt that he could speak to someone in a similar situation again as the impact on him was very positive.

Communication occurs when there are two people getting together and this can be informally or on a more formal basis. We usually form a relationship by exchanging information about ourselves and what is happening within our world.

When we have effective communication skills, we meet our demands for goals at work, and/or at home, also stimulation, entertainment and understanding. We do have a range of skills whereby we can manage our communication, and this is usually subconsciously.

We communicate in many ways such as non-verbal which can be by our body language, eye contact, mannerisms, written such as email and texts and how we write them and if we put pictures and emojis in them. Verbal is speaking which is much clearer.

The skills we have gained to communicate are listening skills and this can be effective by verbal or non-verbal means and here are some examples: -

✓ Lean forward – if you lean forward this is a sign that you would like to be involved in a conversation. You do not feel in a threatened position.

✓ Eye contact - ensure you make good eye contact when you are speaking to people and they will be able to see that you are confident and can be trusted. If you do not make eye contact, this could show that you are hiding something or not being truthful.

✓ Nods of the head – when you nod your head you are acknowledging what the other person is saying and that you are listening intently. This shows that you are interested in the conversation and wish to engage in it.

✓ Facial expressions – your facial expression can so often be a sign if you are unhappy about something. It is important that your facial expression indicates that you are 'tuned in' to the vocal, body and verbal message which is being relayed to you. For example, if someone is unhappy about something, you would not sit and be smiling at them.

✓ Folded arms – can show that you have a protective or separating barrier which can be due to concern or a bit bored. It may be a sign of a subordinate who is feeling threatened by their boss or anyone in authority. Another reason can be if you are feeling cold, but usually this is quite obvious.

✓ Holding papers in front of your chest – this is another protective barrier similar to folded arms.

✓ Hand stroking or supporting your chin - stroking of a beard in men means being thoughtful, although in women it could be supporting the chin.

An American named Professor Albert Mehrabian carried out research which provided the basis for the widely quoted and often much over-simplified statistic for the effectiveness of spoken communications. Below is a representation of Mehrabian's findings:

- 7% of messages pertaining to feelings and attitudes are in the words that are spoken.

- 38% of messages pertaining to feelings and attitudes are paralinguistic (the way that the words are said).

- 55% of messages pertaining to feelings and attitudes are in facial expression.

With effective communication skills, we meet some of our demands which could be achieving goals, self-esteem, understanding and stimulation. Often, we do not think about how we are communicating with each other, but it would be useful for you to spend a couple of minutes around how effective you communicate about a situation you have had or may have in the future, and which methods do you currently use or would use in the future.

Activity

List the methods you find are effective for you and then think if there is anything you may like to change.

Current	Future
1.	1.
2.	2.
3.	3.
4.	4.

Have More Time with Good Organising Skills

I know that I like to be organised, but it is not easy at all. I start the day and I have a list of what I would like to do but something can get in my way or I spend ages looking for a file as I didn't put it back where it should have been. Has this happened or something similar to you?

When you have more than one job to do in any one day, it is a good idea to get yourself organised. It can help you to cope with the world around you when working and trying to have a family life as well. The skills will help to provide a kind of structure, create a semblance of order and they will also reduce daily stress levels.

There are so many things to do, not enough time, so many places to go, lots of people to speak to either in person or on the phone, and so on. Often there is TOO MUCH!

Without good organisational skills to help us cope with busy lives, we would constantly be under pressure and feeling stressed.

Here are some suggestions which I find are useful for not only myself but many people I speak to either at training sessions or when I am coaching them.

To have good organisational skills enables you to save time and as a result free up some valuable time that you can be doing something else or relaxing.

- ✓ Good organisational skills are about having "everything is in its own place and everything has its own place". Try and keep this in mind, then order will be the priority.

- ✓ In the office, at home or at work, prioritise papers in order of importance and put them in a date file. Bills either deal with right away or put in a pending file or drawer, but don't forget about them! Number the files from 1-31 for each day of the week. This worked when I had a PA when I was in the NHS and I still use it each day.

- ✓ When you are going out first thing in the morning, leave your bag plus any important papers near the door and this will make sure that if there are any delays in the morning, you are well prepared. You may not have slept well so this will save time and energy. This can be letters to post or a file. If I don't do this, I will probably forget to take it as I am so used to this being my routine now.

✓ Before going to bed, leave out mugs, bowls and spoons so that breakfast can be prepared with ease. It means that everything is ready, and you can have a relaxed breakfast or a more relaxed one and helps with time.

✓ Reading glasses should be kept in the same place, and an idea is to have a couple of pairs and then you don't spend ages looking for them. If you need glasses when driving, keep a spare pair in the car and it means that they are always at hand. I need to do this as I have had to wear glasses driving since I passed my driving test many years ago.

✓ It does take quite a bit of planning to make sure that you have your duties organised and your own life organised. A diary is very effective and helps your time management, and it is good to jot down what you are going to do, and it is a reminder as well. Once you get into the habit of keeping a diary, it will be something that you can check on a regular basis. Another option is to put important dates down on a calendar in the kitchen where you can always see what is happening over the next month.

✓ Use your mobile phone as an alarm to remind you of certain times when you need to be somewhere, and you can also use the calendar on it as a reminder.

✓ Have a bag with odds and sods in it such as small plastic bags, wipes, hankies, needle and thread, coffee, teabags and when any item is almost finished, then make sure you replenish it. This is useful for me when I go to different offices and I would rather have my own coffee. It is useful to keep the bag in the same place so that you will not forget where it is

Activity - Add to the following example.

Date	Home	Work	Me	Organise

✓ Make lists and prioritise what should be first, second etc and you could do this by a traffic light system; red is urgent, amber is requiring some attention and green means that it can wait for another week. There are only seven days in the week and one of those days should be identified as the day to relax more than the others.

✓ Flexibility is necessary in all that you do as you can otherwise become extremely upset when you may be let down at short notice.

✓ Never feel that you can't cope if you need help, it is better to ask for help and support.

✓ When you cannot be flexible, it is an idea to take a step back and decide what the best option is for you, and this could be that a meeting you were to attend that day has been cancelled and they will let you know when it will be re-arranged with another date and time. This can be extremely frustrating. You could be proactive and suggest another date and time.

Good work/life balance

Balance is the key to making sure that you can have a good work/life balance. It is essential for your physical and psychological wellbeing.

Whether you are a wife, mother, husband, brother, sister - it means that you may have lots of different roles. However, it does mean that you do need to take care of yourself and that you keep yourself fit and healthy.

17

Ways to Improve Your Health

Sustainable exercise you will enjoy and can be part of your daily routine

Taking some form of exercise will help you feel good especially as it increases your heart rate and gets the circulation going in your legs. It is great to do something you like doing and will continue to do.

How about going to an exercise class such as aerobics, spinning class or a dancing class which can be ballroom, salsa or line dancing. Not only will you enjoy the class, but you will also meet other people, and this helps to forget your worries. Any form of exercise is good for us as endorphins are released into the body leaving you with a feel-good feeling.

If you do not fancy going to a class, you could always get a DVD/CD of gentle exercise and practice in the comfort of your own home. Ask some of your friends to come along and make an evening of it.

Be sure that you do not overdo the exercises you undertake, as you don't want to end up with an injury. The best policy is to do something that you not only enjoy but that will be sustainable in the long-term.

At the start of every year, lots of people sign up to a gym membership to get fit but how many continue until the end of that year? I have never done this as I knew that I would never continue – maybe for a few months but that would be it. What I have done in the past is sign up for a few months and that is often enough. There is lots of things you can do without going to the gym such as:

- Running on the spot for five minutes
- Skipping is a good exercise and all you need is a skipping rope
- Ten sit ups which are good for abdomen, hips and thighs
- Weights – small weights for arms and muscles
- Stretching exercises either sitting or standing
- Walk or walk briskly upstairs – don't use the lift unless you have a heavy bag or case!

Some Lifestyle changes

Little changes such as avoiding or reducing coffee, alcohol, cigarettes and drugs (prescribed or over the counter). Instead of having 10 mugs of coffee in a day try to half the amount or have half caffeine coffee and half de-caffeine coffee and see how you get on.

You may enjoy a glass of wine which then can become a whole bottle, how about a miniature bottle or use a small wine glass. Everything is good if in moderation.

Cigarettes are not only bad for your health but for all those around you, so try and reduce and you could go to a Smoking Cessation class. Ask your GP for details. Some people start e-cigarettes but to date there is no definite research as to some of the effects on your health. Ideally, it is best to stop smoking completely or at least cut down slowly.

When you are busy, food can become a dilemma as you will either be eating too much of maybe the wrong foods such as fried foods, takeaways and food high in fat and in calories. On the other hand, you may not have much of an appetite and could be losing weight, so in this instance ensure that you are eating three meals in a day and that they contain fresh fruit and vegetables and enough calories to increase your weight. If in any doubt, ask your GP to give you a diet which will suit you.

I was at a local office recently and most of the staff were working in an open plan area. Almost everyone had a cup or mug on their desk with some sort of drink in it whether hot or cold.

There were water fountains they could use as well as hot water. I know when I go to this office that I don't need to take a bottle of water with me which is less to carry as well.

Relax and have a cuppa...

You can have tea and there are many different types you can get either as loose tea or tea bags.

Here is one suggestion, but you can try your own options.

Fresh Mint and Ginger Tea Recipe

1-1½ heaped teaspoons of green tea leaves
2-4 sprigs of fresh mint (with or without the stems)
3-6 zest of an orange
½ teaspoon of chopped ginger root

Sugar or small quantity of honey to taste

Put into a teapot or cafetière and add boiling water for 2-3 cups.

Allow to stand for a minute or two, stir and serve.

Enjoy........

18

Activities, Quiz, Questionnaires

Stress/Worry Diary

Identify dates and times over one week to see if there is a pattern when you are feeling under pressure or worrying which is causing signs and symptoms of stress.

There is one example.

In the middle column, indicate how you feel:-

	Stressed
	Under some pressure
	Feeling better/improvement

Monday			Tuesday		
Time	Stressor and Reaction	Me	Time	Stressor and Reaction	Me
09.00	My boss, tension in shoulders, neck.	☹	08.30	No support today, tearful, annoyed	☹

Wednesday			Thursday		
Time	Stressor and Reaction	Me	Time	Stressor and Reaction	Me

Friday			Saturday/Sunday		
Time	Stressor and Reaction	Me	Time	Stressor and Reaction	Me

At end of week total number:

☹	
😐	
🙂	

Jessica M Smyrl

Monday			Tuesday		
Time	Stressor and Reaction	Me	Time	Stressor and Reaction	Me

Wednesday			Thursday		
Time	Stressor and Reaction	Me	Time	Stressor and Reaction	Me

Friday			Saturday/Sunday		
Time	Stressor and Reaction	Me	Time	Stressor and Reaction	Me

At end of week total number:

Complete the Stress Diary and then identify what changes you will make in your life.

Example: Scenario.

1. Look for another job in a different department or area.

2. Speak to X and let him/her know exactly how you feel; they may be completely unaware of their reaction as they could be starting to show signs of stress in their behaviour and becoming more aggressive.

3. Have a word with your line manager.

4. Discuss with a colleague.

5. Do nothing.

6. Ignore X.

7. Speak to friend/colleague/counsellor to have regular support.

8. Agree best way forward for you.

YOU have more power to change around you.

Activity – Make a list of priorities and put them in order of importance of how to improve the situation.

1.

2.

3.

4.

5.

6.

7.

8.

9.

10.

Causes of Stress – write down below what is causing your stress. Put it in one colour and try again in a few months' time and see if there is any difference.

Identify what is causing you to be stressed

Write in the date as this may give you a pattern, but if not just write when you think it was. After completing, then go to the Action Plan.

What causes your pressure and how you react such as getting angry, tense or tearful?

Date	Cause of Stress or Pressure	How do you React?

Activity - Relaxation

This helpful activity can be used as part of a stress management programme when feeling stressed or under pressure. The activity encourages a proactive approach to problem solving and therefore can effectively reduce stress levels.

Think of some ways to reduce or stop the main sources of stress in your personal or working life.

What You Need

✓ Three small cards or pieces of paper
✓ Pen

• Write down 1 major cause of stress in your life on each card or piece of paper. Take a few minutes to do this activity.

• Take 5-10 minutes to come up with 3 possible solutions for each cause of your stress.

• What did you learn from carrying out this activity?

• Did you have some of the causes of stress listed earlier in the book?

• How will you deal with them and when will you get started?

Activity – Create relaxation just for you

You require four or five common objects which can be used to help you relax. These can be a small pillow or cushion, piece of paper, a clock with a second hand, a pencil, a photo from a magazine of a beach scene and a coloured drawing-pin.

✓ Small pillow or cushion – place on a chair in the small of your back or put it under your head.

✓ Paper – for drawing, scribbling or as a visualisation exercise

✓ Clock/watch with a second hand – to time a relaxation exercise or focus on the second hand to relax and unwind.

✓ Pencil – as an aid in an eye-movement exercise or for drawing or scribbling.

✓ Photo from a magazine of a beach scene – to visualise a pleasant scene before relaxing.

✓ Coloured drawing pin – can be used as a focal point to relax when carrying out breathing exercises.

Lie down on the floor or somewhere comfortable and relax.

Do this as often as you feel and somewhere quiet away from any noise or distraction.

Activity - Quick de-stress

How to relax when dealing with an ongoing stressful situation

A normal reaction to a stressful situation is to feel worried or even to feel in a panic. Try to stay calm and to assess and react to the situation by asking yourself 'What am I trying to achieve'. The following techniques will help you focus better: -

Breathe – deeply and slowly to slow down the brain waves and to convert from the fight/flight response to the relaxation response.

Talk – to an individual, friend(s) or colleague(s). When you talk to someone this can help to offload any distress. Remember excess dis-stress causes dis-ease, leading to illness.

Exercise – Deep breathing and sunshine decreases your adrenaline build up, increases your mental awareness by more oxygen going to the brain and this helps you think and function much better. Take a walk around the block or in the garden.

Diet – look at your diet and avoid stimulants, especially coffee, excess strong tea, alcohol and white sugar. Eat fruit regularly to keep your brain glucose levels up. Drink 8 medium glasses of water a day.

When really stressed keep a routine and build into your life 'ME TIME' time to relax, eat, get enough sleep, as well as rewarding yourself daily for all your hard work.

Relaxation method

Sit in a comfortable chair: -

✓Begin by clenching your right hand, make a fist, make it tight, notice the sensation of tension in the hand and forearm while you hold it for 5 seconds, then let it go, feel the hand and forearm becoming relaxed and comfortable, warm and relaxed, relaxed and heavy.
Continue doing the same, of tense and release below and then relax for 10-15 minutes.

✓ Clench the left hand and release it
✓ raise the eyebrows and release them
✓ wrinkle the forehead and release it
✓ frown and release
✓ screw your eyes up tight and release them
✓ bite your teeth together and release
✓ press your lips together and release them
✓ press your head against the back of the chair then relax
✓ press your chin down on to your chest and relax it
✓ hunch your shoulders up to your ears and relax them
✓ pull your stomach in and tense the muscles and then release
✓ arch your back so that your spine leaves the back of the chair and then relax it
✓ tense your buttock muscles and relax
✓ tighten your toes and relax them

Relax for 10-15 minutes and slowly become aware of your surroundings and then slowly sit forward and stand up. Take a drink of water to refresh and make you feel energised.

Activity - Make a fist

✓ Make a fist with your right hand and hold for 5 seconds and then let your hand and arm flop and relax it.

✓ Make a fist with your left hand and hold for 5 seconds and then let your hand and arm flop and relax it.

This helps to reduce tension in hands, arms and shoulders. Try this anytime you feel tense and keep repeating until you feel more relaxed. This is my number one tip and I check my hands on a regular basis as often we don't realise that we are under stress. I always mention about this tip at training sessions because I know it does work and costs nothing – just need to remember to do it from time to time.

Breathing Exercise – this is a quick relaxation when you are feeling stressed, anxious, panic or fearful and worried.

Place one hand on your abdomen and one on your chest. As you inhale, and exhale note the movement of your abdomen and chest. If you are breathing correctly the hand on your abdomen should rise as you breathe in. Therefore, if your hand is stationery on your abdomen then you are breathing incorrectly.

Relaxed breathing can be a powerful and natural antidote to stress. Many people who take the time to change the way they breathe say they experience a greater rest, relaxation and ease.
Try this at home and practice.

Action Plan

Firstly, identify what is causing you to be stressed and then write down what and if you are using any techniques to reduce stress and this could be bad methods such as smoking, drinking or maybe not doing anything at all.

After going through the book have a think about what techniques or skills you will start and this could be becoming more organised and having more time for 'me'. You can do it so, how about starting now.

What is causing your stress?	Techniques and skills currently used	Techniques and skills to change or improve

1. Identify stressors e.g. changing the environment, improving relationships, setting priorities
2. Self-knowledge of how you react
3. Techniques and skills currently used, if any e.g. smoking, walking
4. Techniques and skills to change or improve e.g. eat healthily, more exercise

GOAL SETTING - SHORT TERM GOALS

Look at what you have written down on the Action Plan and start from there. You don't need to have three goals to begin with. Try with one and then work your way through to adding when you feel able.

Just think about yourself and how important you are. It is vital that you keep fit and healthy so putting some time aside for yourself is of great importance to you.

Tip - Start from 1 week to 3 months but start at a week, then a month at a time. Try with small steps and small goals right now.

What would you like to spend more time doing or to start doing? This could be joining a class or going out a bit more even for a short time. Each step is a positive message to improving your lifestyle and health.

1.

2.

3.

What would you like to spend less time doing?

Some examples could be eating on your own or being on your own.

1.

2.

3.

List some actions you could take now to start these goals. An example could be keep a diary or one day for relaxing.

Remember – make sure that they are realistic ones!

1.

2.

3.

Start them today!

Write down some positive thoughts or turn negatives to positives.

Positive Notes:

Activity – try this quiz.

ARE YOU UNDER STRESS?

The symptoms of stress can range from vague feelings of anxiety to lowered resistance to disease. On this page is an easy test you can take to see how much stress you may be under.

Check your symptoms, give yourself a score for only those items that apply, a 1 indicates the item is not stressful; a 5 indicates that it is very stressful.

Add the scores in each category, and then total your scores for past and future.
If an item below affected you in the last six months, circle the number that describes the amount of stressed it caused you.

1 2 3 4 5   1. Feeling that things or life are
                        getting out of control

1 2 3 4 5   2. Anxiety or panic attacks

1 2 3 4 5   3. Frustration

1 2 3 4 5   4. Angry and irritated

1 2 3 4 5   5. Feeling desperate, hopeless

1 2 3 4 5   6. Feeling trapped, helpless

1 2 3 4 5   7. Feeling depressed

1 2 3 4 5   8. Feeling guilty

1 2 3 4 5   9. Feeling self-conscious

1 2 3 4 5   10. Feeling restless

Score = _____

If your total is 15 or below, you need not be concerned about stress.

If your score is over 15, then you may be under a moderate amount of stress.

If your score is more than 27, you should be concerned and find some effective ways of managing stress.

One Small Change

All you need to do is to make one small change and this could make you feel great and to improve your life and wellbeing.

Action

What are you going to do differently after you have read this book?

You have more control than you think.

Final thoughts and Tips for You

"Things do not change. We change." –
Henry David Thoreau

Tip 1 - Yes you can change and yes you can make it happen.

The main thing is for you to be positive and keep saying to yourself "yes I can do it" and "yes I will try".

I do this on a regular basis when I doubt myself, I just think well hold on, I did this before, so I will do it again and keep saying to myself that I will. Start your day with saying a positive thought that today is going to be a good or even a great day and remind yourself with writing down on a piece of paper or a sticky note.

Tip 2 - Look at yourself in the mirror, even when you do not feel great and keep saying to your reflection that you can and will change.

We have all heard that 'a leopard won't change its spots' but the change you wish to make is how you feel about yourself and look yourself in the eyes in the mirror and say that you are going to change by putting on brighter clothes, for example, today. No dark clothes and this helps you feel a whole lot better.

I was speaking with an employee in a local company and he always wore white or dare I say off-white shirts. I said to him on a regular basis over the years about wearing a coloured shirt and tie. It took him at least three years to wear a coloured shirt but what a difference it made to his overall outlook on life and he felt happier in himself.

Tip 3 - You cannot change the fact that you are feeling stressed, but what you can do is look at what you have control over and can change.

Everyone has something different in life where they can make a small change. Some days when I went into the office in the morning there was no milk or coffee, so instead of getting stressed and annoyed about it, I decided to have my own supply just in case. This has made me feel more relaxed.

The Chief Executive of a company had a PA who was very stressed a lot of the time and I was asked to have a word with her. What was causing her to get very stressed was that there was a shared printer in the middle of an open plan office which she had to use. A lot of her documents were urgent and when her boss was shouting for documents she couldn't get them to him quick enough as there was a queue of documents being printed every time she went to the printer. After speaking with her, I suggested that the solution was to get a printer in her office for her use only. When I saw her a couple of weeks later, she felt great as she no longer was under excessive pressure and documents were ready when she needed them.

Tip 4 - One thing can make a huge difference to you.

This could be by giving yourself a small treat at least once a week. How about taking an afternoon or evening off and doing something that you really enjoy doing either on your own or with others. The choice is yours.

Tip 5 - The key to fighting stress is just one small step and one change at a time.

That is right and there may be one thing in this book which you think will work for you so try it and see. It could be getting to bed at the same time each night which I now do most of the time. This allows me to have a good night's sleep. If you are worried about something, then have a notepad beside the bed and write down your worries or make a list of what you are to do the next day.

Think of little changes you would like to take, and this can make a big difference and then decide which one you can change TODAY.

Tip 6 – Take time out.

Be sure to make time for you away from the hustle and bustle of daily life. Diary in breaks, some downtime, or play time in your day. Taking time for yourself can help relieve stress and refresh you so you can do a lot more.

Tip 7 – Release the tension

This is a great activity of a simple yoga stretch for releasing muscle tension which can be due to stress. It takes just a few minutes and see how you feel afterwards.

- Stand relaxed, arms hanging at your sides and your feet about one foot apart.

- Tilt your head back and hold for five seconds

- Then roll your head forward and hold for five seconds.

- Curl your chest and stomach forward as you bend at the waist and let arms flop for five seconds.

- Inhale slowly through your mouth as you straighten up.

- Raise your arms up above your head and then let arms go slowly to your sides as you exhale slowly though your mouth.

Tip 8 - Laughing will help to reduce stress, make you feel good, and reduce muscle tension.

There are laughter yoga classes locally which I have been told are very good. Even if you do not wish to go to a class, then check it out on YouTube which you can see how it is done or just try and do it yourself.

Tip 9 - You are the one who has the control to make things happen.

Yes, it is you and you alone who can make things happen. Do not doubt yourself, be positive and say yes, I will do this as it will make me feel better in myself and about myself and no one will stop me. The more you say these words the more you will believe, and I know you can and will do it so get on and do it.

To aim to feel great, how about giving a try to these tips

✓ Yes, you can change and yes you can make it happen.

✓ Look at yourself in the mirror, even when you do not feel great and keep saying to your reflection that you can and will change.

✓ You cannot change the fact that you are feeling stressed, but what you can do is look at what you have control over and can change.

✓ One thing can make a huge difference to you.

✓ The key to fighting stress is just one small step and one change at a time.

✓ Take time out.

✓ Release the tension.

✓ Laughing will help to reduce stress, make you feel good, and reduce muscle tension.

✓ You are the one who has the control to make things happen.

✓ Start today! Don't put it off.

☺ . . . .

☺ . . . .

☺ . . . .

☺ . . . .

☺ . . . .

☺ . . . .

☺ . . . .

☺ . . . .

Changes you will now make are....

Useful contacts

There are some contact details which could be of benefit to you.

Alcoholics Anonymous
www.alcoholics-anonymous.org.uk
Helpline: 0845 769 7555
AA is a society of people recovering from alcohol abuse.

Alzheimer's Society
Alzheimer's Society is a membership organisation, which works to improve the quality of life of people affected by dementia in England, Wales and Northern Ireland.
Tel: 020 7423 3500
Email: enquiries@alzheimers.org.uk
Website: www.alzheimers.org.uk

Alzheimer Scotland
Alzheimer Scotland for people with dementia, those who care for them and anyone with a concern or query regarding dementia.
Tel: 0808 808 3000
Email: alzheimer@alzscot.org
Website: www.alzscot.org

American Institute of Stress
A good American site, with limited free information, however, there is lots of information packs etc. are available for sale.
www.stress.org

Anxiety UK
ANXIETY UK works to relieve and support those living with anxiety disorders by providing information, support and understanding via an extensive range of services.
Tel: 0161 227 9898
Email: info@anxietyuk.org.uk
Website: www.anxietyuk.org.uk

Association for Coaching
A membership association for Professional Coaches and Organisations.
Email: enquiries@associationforcoaching.com
Website: www.associationforcoaching.com

British Association for Counselling and Psychotherapy
Lists of qualified counsellors and psychotherapists available.
Tel: 0870 443 5252
Email: babcp@babcp.co.uk
Website: www.bacp.co.uk

Breathing Space Scotland
Free, confidential phone line you can call when you're feeling down.
Helpline: 0800 838587
Email: info@breathingspacescotland.co.uk
Website: www.breathingspacescotland.co.uk

The British Psychological Society
The British Psychological Society is the representative body for psychology and psychologists in the UK.
Tel: 0116 254 9568
E-mail: enquiries@bps.org.uk
Website: www.bps.org.uk

CALL Helpline Wales
Confidential listening and support service for people in Wales.
Tel: 0800 132737
Website: www.callhelpline.org.uk

Carers UK
Information and help for the UK's six million carers.
Tel: 020 7490 8818   Carers line: 0808 808 7777
Email: info@carersuk.org
Website: www.carersuk.org

Carers Link East Dunbartonshire
Carers Link is a local organisation dedicated to Carers providing a range of services for people who live or care within the East Dunbartonshire area.
Tel: 0800 975 2131
Email: enquiry@carerslink.org.uk
Website: www.carerslink.org.uk

Carers Northern Ireland
Tel: 028 9043 9843
Email: info@carersni.org
Website: www.carersni.org

Carers Scotland
Tel: 0141 445 3070
Email: info@carerscotland.org
Website: www.carerscotland.org

Carers Wales
Tel: 029 2081 1370
Email: info@carerswales.org
Website: www.carerswales.org

CAUSE (Carers and Users Support Enterprise)
Northern Ireland charity providing practical and emotional support to relatives and carers of people with mental illness.
Tel: 028 9023 8284
Email: info@cause.org.uk
Website: www.cause.org.uk

Childstress.com
This is for children and parents, provides information about stress in children and offers tips and ideas on how to reduce it.
www.childstress.com

Chipmunkapublishing.com
Chipmunka Publishing is the Mental Health Publisher. Their mental health books give a voice to writers with mental illness around the world. Most of their mental health books are written by people with mental health issues.
Email: info@chipmunkapublishing.com
Website: www.chipmunkapublishing.com

Eyegaze

Stress is a factor in everybody's life but Deaf people more commonly experience depression and anxiety and other inevitable stress associated with being Deaf in a world geared towards the needs of hearing people.

www.eyegaze.tv

Grow Community Mental Health

GROW in Ireland is a worldwide community mental health movement with over 140 groups throughout Ireland.

Tel (ROI): 1890 474 474

Web site www.grow.ie

Health And Safety Authority

(Note: Irish equivalent to HSE) Advice for Work Related Stress Contact Information:

Tel. No.: (01) 614 7000,

Web Site: www.hsa.ie

Health & Safety Executive

The Health and Safety Commission is responsible for health and safety regulation in Great Britain. The Health and Safety Executive and local government are the enforcing authorities who work in support of the Commission.

Tel: 020 7224 1539

Website: www.hse.gov.uk/stress/index.htm

ISMA^{UK} (International Stress Management Association)

ISMA^{UK} is a registered charity with a multi-disciplinary professional membership that includes the UK and the Republic of Ireland. It exists to promote sound knowledge and best practice in the prevention and reduction of human stress. It sets professional standards for the benefit of individuals and organisations using the services of its members.
Tel: 01179 697 284
Email: stress@isma.org.uk
Website: www.isma.org.uk

Mental Health Ireland

Mental Health Ireland is a national voluntary organisation which aims to promote positive mental health.
Tel: 01-2841166
Web: www.mentalhealthireland.ie

Mind

Offers many services including helplines, drop-in centres, supported housing, counselling, befriending, advocacy, and employment and training schemes.
Information line: 0845 766 0163
Email: contact@mind.org.uk
Website: www.mind.org.uk

National Collaborating Centre for Mental Health

Offers accessible information on NICE mental health guidelines.
Website: www.nccmh.org.uk

National Stress Awareness Day - first Wednesday in November every year in the UK
Email: nsad@isma.org.uk
Website: www.nsad.org.uk

NHS Choices
This is the primary public facing website of the NHS. Its pages include directories of local health services (a Directory of Services), information on a wide range of conditions and treatments and accessible public health information.
Website: www.nhs.uk/

NHS24
This is the website of the National Health Service advice service in Scotland. There are Sections on stress, anxiety and depression.
www.nhs24.scot.nhs.uk

Northern Ireland Association for Mental Health
Provides local support, including housing schemes, home support, advocacy services and information, for those with mental health needs.
Tel: 028 9032 8474
Email: edassistant@niamh.org.uk
Website: www.niamh.co.uk

Sane
Offers information, crisis care and emotional support.
Helpline: 0845 767 8000
Email: info@sane.org.uk
Website: www.sane.org.uk
Scottish Association for Mental Health

Campaigns and provides services across Scotland for people with mental health problems, homelessness, addictions and other forms of social exclusion.
Tel: 0141 568 7000
Email: enquiries@samh.org.uk
Website: www.samh.org.uk

www.stressassistance.co.uk
Stress cards, stress balls, stress markers, stress diary, downloads online shop
Email: orders@stressassistance.co.uk

www.yourstressmanagement.co.uk
Stress consultancy, risk, audit and training. Available world-wide as well as speaking.

Bibliography

Alexander, F N (1932) The use of the self, Dutton, New York

Armstrong, K F (1972) Anatomy & Physiology for Nurses, Bailliere Tindall, London

Beck, Mary E (1962) Churchill Livingstone, Edinburgh

Benson, H (1976) The Relaxation Response, Collins, London

Cheung, T (2008) 100 Ways to Boost Your Immune System, Harper Collins

Cooper, C L and Palmer, S (2000) Conquer Your Stress, CIPD

Epstein, R (2000) The Big Book of Stress Relief Games, McGraw Hill, New York

Health and Safety Executive (HSE) 2001 Tackling Work-Related Stress: A managers' guide to improving and maintaining employee health and well-being, HSE, Suffolk

Jacobson, E (1938) Progressive relaxation, 2nd edn. University of Chicago Press, Chicago

Lichstein, K L (1988) Clinical relaxation strategies, John Wiley, New York

Mitchell (1987) Simple relaxation: the Mitchell method for easing tension, 2nd edn, John Murray, London

Ost, L G (1987), Applied relaxation: description of a coping technique and review of controlled studies. Behaviour Research and Therapy 25:397-407

Palmer, S and Cooper, C L (2007) How to Deal with Stress, Kogan Page, London

Poppen R, (1988) Behavioural relaxation training and assessment, Pergamon Press, Oxford

Quilliam, S (2003) Positive Thinking, Dorling Kindersley, London

Weil, A (2000) Eating well for optimum health, Sphere, London

Carnegie, Dale How To Stop Worrying And Start Living, Cedar; 1993 Edition

Websites
www.hse.gov.uk/stress
www.isma.org.uk
www.businessballs.com
www.cipd.co.uk
www.mind.org.uk
www.nhs.uk/